Writing Nonfiction

A SIMPLE, CLEAR APPROACH FOR HIGH SCHOOLERS

Writing Nonfiction

A SIMPLE, CLEAR APPROACH FOR HIGH SCHOOLERS

HERON BOOKS

Heron Books, Inc.
20950 SW Rock Creek Road
Sheridan, OR 97378

heronbooks.com

Special thanks to all the teachers and students who
provided feedback instrumental to this edition.

First Edition © 2020, 2023 Heron Books
All Rights Reserved

ISBN: 978-0-89-739183-2

Any unauthorized copying, translation, duplication or distribution, in whole
or in part, by any means, including electronic copying, storage or transmission,
is a violation of applicable laws.

The Heron Books name and the heron bird symbol are registered
trademarks of Delphi Schools, Inc.

Printed in the USA

4 August 2023

At Heron Books, we think learning should be engaging and fun. It should be hands-on and allow students to move at their own pace.

To facilitate this, we have created a learning guide that will help any student progress through this book, chapter by chapter, with confidence and interest.

Get learning guides at
heronbooks.com/learningguides.

For a final exam, email
teacherresources@heronbooks.com

We would love to hear from you!
Email us at feedback@heronbooks.com.

CONTENTS

Introduction 1

Part 1
The Seven Steps

1 Step One: Know Your Purpose 5

2 Step Two: Define Your Audience 7

3 Step Three: Organize Your Thoughts 9

4 Step Four: Write a Draft 11

5 Step Five: Revise and Refine 13

6 Step Six: Use Feedback 17

7 Step Seven: Finish the Piece 21

Part 2
The Parts

8 Words 27

9 Sentences 31

10 Paragraphs 39

11 Sections 43

Part 3
The Types

12 Persuasive 49

13 Personal 55

14 Business 57

15 Academic 61

Part 4
Tools and Tips

16 Tone 75

17 Consistency 77

18 Active vs. Passive 81

19 Concrete Language 85

20 Usage Tips 89

Part 5
Clarity and Style

21 Four Enemies of Clarity 103

22 Developing a Style 107

Reference Section

Common Standards & Usage Samples 111
Glossary 123
Index 131

VII

INTRODUCTION

Nonfiction writing is about real people, real places, real events. It can come in many forms: books, essays, articles, blogs, reports, proposals, short stories, biographies, autobiographies, scientific or other technical papers, and more.

Many young writers believe that creative writing is fun and interesting, while nonfiction writing is dry and boring. This is not true. Just as a painter may view a certain scene and capture it on canvas in a striking, unique and beautiful way, so can a writer of nonfiction capture reality in a way that is unique, creative, and even inspiring.

The book *Night* by Elie Wiesel is a memoir[1] of the author's experience in Nazi concentration camps at the height of the Holocaust. The writing (as translated into English) is sparse and unadorned, plain and painfully factual, not unlike a black-and-white movie documentary. But its creative force, its sheer vitality and power, has made it one of the most important books ever written on the terrors of the Holocaust. As nonfiction, it is both horrifying and inspiring.

One expects nonfiction writing to be accurate, informative and analytical. But it can also be imaginative, emotional, even awe-inspiring. *It can be anything communication can be.*

With twenty-two short chapters and an extensive reference section, *Writing Nonfiction* was created to help you say the things you want to say clearly and effectively.

Ready? Let's get started!

---

1 **memoir:** a type of biography or autobiography that usually covers a select time period in the person's life as remembered by the writer.

Part 1

THE SEVEN STEPS

This section describes seven essential steps to writing a great piece of nonfiction writing.

STEP ONE: KNOW YOUR PURPOSE

The usual goal of a piece[1] of nonfiction writing is to inform the reader.

This may seem obvious, but even the best writers of nonfiction can get caught up in the writing and forget that the reader is expecting to be *informed*.

Beyond that, however, each piece of writing will have a purpose that is more specific than the general goal of informing. You will want to work out what this purpose is before you start writing. It will get you started on the right track and help keep you on the right track as you are organizing your thoughts.

For example, you may want to introduce a particular viewpoint on a topic, one you believe will be new to the reader.

You may want to persuade your reader toward some decision or action.

You may want to document or recreate some event, making the reader feel as if they experienced it themselves.

Or you may want to present a series of facts that lead to a particular conclusion.

Though often informal and probably not something you've considered nonfiction writing, a friendly letter, email or blog post usually has the

---

1 **piece:** A single creation of art, music or writing. In writing, a *piece* can be an essay, an article or any other composition. For example, "This piece on space travel is very informative and well-written," or "She wrote a lengthy piece on the history of women's soccer in Brazil." The term *piece* is used throughout this book as a general term for whatever kind of nonfiction writing you may be doing. It was chosen instead of the word *composition* because it implies more personal creativity and is used more commonly for professional work.

PART 1 THE SEVEN STEPS

purpose of keeping someone informed on how and what you are doing in life. It is a common form of nonfiction writing.

Letters, emails or posts of any length may also have the specific purpose of expressing gratitude or other emotions, or inviting people to some activity being planned. They usually have a specific purpose. When they don't, they are usually not as enjoyable to read because they tend to wander without delivering any clear message.

Another type of nonfiction writing concerns the writing of reports. By definition, a **report** is a description or telling about something that happened or the results of investigation. Again, the goal is to inform, but the purpose of a report should be more specific, such as giving the reader a more accurate view into some subject or event, or presenting facts in a certain way that point to what's important about them or what conclusions you have drawn from them.

Research reports often have the added purpose of answering the specific questions of a research assignment or question that you or another posed[2] before you began the research.

These are just examples to illustrate the importance of knowing what your purpose is before you start organizing a piece of nonfiction writing.

> *Clarifying the purpose of a piece will make it easier to write and more enjoyable to read.*

---

2 **pose:** to present (a problem or situation) or ask (a question) for discussion or consideration. For example, "She *posed* a question for the team to discuss," or "The essay assignment *posed* a set of questions for the student to consider and discuss in writing."

STEP TWO: DEFINE YOUR AUDIENCE

The person or type of people you are writing to matters. Think about how you might tell the same story to your grandfather, your six-year-old sister, your teacher, or your best friend. There would certainly be differences!

Before writing, define your audience. It will affect your choice of words, sentence length, the kind of examples used, how you interest the reader, how you organize the ideas. It will even affect whether or not the use of humor will be appropriate and what will be humorous to that audience.

Writing for someone who already agrees with you is quite different from writing for someone whose viewpoint you are trying to change.

If you're sharing an interesting story with friends, your descriptions might be more colorful or informal than if you're writing a report about the same event for school.

If you have done extensive research on a subject, you might take extra care with how you introduce the subject to someone who may not be familiar with the terminology or other details you now take for granted.

To be sure your communication actually arrives, define your audience before starting any writing.

STEP THREE: ORGANIZE YOUR THOUGHTS

The next step in putting together a piece of nonfiction writing is creating some sort of plan or guide for the piece.

Whether worked out in detail or sketched out as a general plan, this organizing step is normally called creating an outline. Even in a short piece of writing where the organizing step is done in your head, you're still working out some sort of outline, like this:

1. attract the reader and let them know where you're going,

2. first point with examples,

3. second point with examples,

4. third and most important point with examples,

5. destination/conclusion/wrap-up.

Though simple, it could help save you quite a bit of time.

An outline will be especially useful in developing a more complex piece of writing. You can ensure your flow of ideas is logical, spot missing steps or arguments, gain better insight into your purpose and how to achieve it, and much more.

A well-done outline should give you a good framework so you can start rolling on the writing—and hopefully avoid getting into a tangle half-way through.

Here are some organizing tips you may find useful for a larger piece:

- When starting, you may have various different ideas. Make a diagram or sketch of them.
- Note what you want to say about each of them.

PART 1 THE SEVEN STEPS

- Group them into categories if helpful.
- Draw arrows showing how they might best flow one to the next.
- Look it over and see what's missing or unnecessary to the purpose.
- Always be willing to change the outline, even as you're writing. An outline is nothing more than a tool to help you communicate effectively!

These are tips, not rules. With experience, you'll learn what works best in organizing your thoughts before you launch into writing.

Occasionally, an instructor may ask for your outline, either before you write the piece or with the piece itself. Know what sort of format or style the instructor wants, if any.[3]

Usually, writing instructors request outlines as a way to help you learn to organize your thoughts and learn to discipline your thinking and writing. Often they will stop requesting them once they know you are good at organizing your thoughts and writing papers that flow logically and don't jump around in a way that is hard to follow.

Outlines are useful for more than school assignments. As a professional, you may be asked to provide an outline for a proposal, speech or presentation before creating or presenting it. You may even find it useful to provide an outline at the beginning of a presentation.

Outlining is a useful skill to master.

> *Getting good at organizing your thoughts with outlines*
> *can dramatically change your ability to*
> *write great nonfiction pieces.*

---

[3] Sample outlines are provided in the reference section at the back of the book.

STEP FOUR: WRITE A DRAFT

Once you have your ideas organized, start writing. This will be your first draft, the first version of a piece of writing before any revising is done.

To get started, many writing instructors recommend that you write without stopping to correct errors. If this works for you, great. If this doesn't work for you, do whatever works to keep the flow of writing going.

If you find yourself struggling to get started, here are a few tips:

- Check your interest. If you aren't interested in the topic, you need to backtrack and find out why. Until you are genuinely interested, there's little chance your writing will be good.
- Recheck the earlier steps. If you glossed over your purpose, audience or outline, it can trip you up when you have to start writing your first draft.
- Don't get stuck on writing the perfect first paragraph or two. Because of their importance, most writers give more attention to the opening and closing paragraphs later on in the process of developing the piece. For now, just get something down.
- Trust your outline and follow it.

Even for the best writers, a great piece of writing rarely occurs on the first draft.

Your goal for the first draft should be to create something you can then develop into a great piece.

STEP FIVE:
REVISE AND REFINE

What if you like your first draft? You might think, "Great. I'm done."

It's certainly better to have a first draft that you like than one you don't. But a good first draft simply means you have something good to work with, something with a better chance of turning into a great piece!

It's like a good first half of a sports game. You're ahead, and things are looking good to get the win. But if you decide the game is won and loaf through the second half, you lose. Or think of it like a concert or play that has reached intermission with the audience wanting more. The part of the performance that comes after the intermission, done well, can ensure the show is a rave success!

It's what you do *after* you've written a good draft that takes your good writing and makes it great. And that's done by revising and refining.

If you take a fresh look at your first draft, particularly from the viewpoint of your reader, you will begin to see ways to improve it. Ask yourself:

- Is it logical in the flow of ideas?
- Is it confusing anywhere?
- Does it use a lot more words than are needed?
- Is it boring and lacking specifics?
- Is the overall message unclear?

Reading it aloud can sometimes help you spot these things more easily.

PART 1 THE SEVEN STEPS

Revising means examining and changing your writing to improve it.

You will normally start with big changes, such as changing paragraph order to improve the logical flow, adding sentences or paragraphs or sections to provide information that you now see was needed, or deleting parts that seem redundant.

If you start with changes to small details, you may end up spending time on things that will be moved around or deleted later. So, try to address the larger problems first.

With the purpose and audience for your paper in mind, do the following until you are sure you have said what you want to say, the way you want to say it.

- ADD
  Sometimes adding data will clarify your point. Perhaps you left a thought only half-explained or the connection between two paragraphs is missing.

- DELETE
  A first draft often has unnecessary words, sentences or paragraphs that can be deleted. For example, you are revising and see sentences or paragraphs that repeat something already stated, or you see a sentence where the same thing can be said in fewer words.

- CHANGE THE ORDER
  As you read your writing, it may become clear that changing the order of sentences or paragraphs will make the piece more logical. You want the reader to be able to move easily from one thought or idea to the next.

- REPLACE
  To say exactly what you intend, you can replace inaccurate or confusing words or sentences with ones that say exactly what you mean.

After you are satisfied with your revisions, you can improve it further by refining it.

PART 1 THE SEVEN STEPS

Refining your writing means making more detailed changes to sharpen the writing.

The idea of refining is to "purify" your writing of any illogical or inexact ideas, wordiness, and so on. Refined writing is clear and enjoyable to read.

You can refine a piece using the same actions as revising—add, delete, change the order, replace. However, the changes are made to rid the piece of the last few impurities, such as

- adding a missing transition[4];
- tightening a sentence by deleting unnecessary words;
- smoothing out places where the writing does not flow;
- replacing a word or phrase with a more exact one.

Revising and refining are not exact processes. It may happen that you think you have made all the big revisions needed and have spent further time refining a piece. Then while reading your paper again, you realize you left out a major point. You should write the paragraph (or paragraphs) to make that point and add it to your paper, then newly revise and refine to make sure everything fits together well.

Continue revising and refining to achieve your overall purpose and a standard[5] you feel good about. With practice, you'll get better and faster at it.

> *Only when you are satisfied the writing has met your standard should you consider the piece ready to be read.*

---

4 **transition**: a word or group of words that helps connect sentences or paragraphs together, such as *thus, however, for this reason*, or *because of this*. (For more examples, see the reference section at the back of the book.)

5 **standard**: a level of quality, particularly one that is well accepted.

STEP SIX: USE FEEDBACK

Part of writing well is learning how clearly your readers understand what you have written and what they think you are trying to say. This means sharing your writing with others so they can give you feedback.

Feedback is information on how well you are doing something for the purpose of improving performance.

Feedback on a piece of writing would be what someone has to say about how well your writing communicates, what was understandable, effective, confusing or unclear. It may or may not include suggestions for improvement, depending on the circumstances.

In educational settings, feedback from others, such as fellow students, is sometimes allowed, sometimes not. When allowed, there may be restrictions on what is allowed. For example, an instructor may allow feedback with suggestions, but only if the suggestions refer to the course text. This helps ensure good training on the information of the course and prevents opinions or confusions from spreading. But even simple feedback without suggestions can say whether or not the piece was easy to read and communicated clearly, which can be very helpful.

If someone is tasked with the specific responsibility of helping you on your writing, the feedback will be expected to be more detailed and instructive.

PART 1 THE SEVEN STEPS

Tips for Coaches[6]

For those coaching others on their writing, some tips are presented here, as they can be useful to both the coach and the student receiving the feedback.

- UNDERSTAND AND ACKNOWLEDGE
  Receive and understand the writer's message and acknowledge it. This may seem obvious, but sometimes a coach gets caught up in spotting errors and forgets to receive, understand and give an acknowledgment to the writer.

- ENCOURAGE
  Coach with an encouraging attitude. Part of this is commenting on the writing, not the writer, and doing so in a constructive way.

- ASK, DON'T TELL
  When the writing isn't clear, ask for clarification as opposed to saying what you think should have been written. For example, "Is this sentence missing something?" or "I didn't get the connection between these two paragraphs."

- FOCUS
  Rather than directing attention to a variety of things, try to focus on the one writing point or skill that seems to need the most attention. This helps the writer improve one ability at a time.

- CORRECT
  Having someone return a paper with a lot of errors marked is not actually that helpful. As much as possible, when correcting a piece of writing, direct the writer's attention to trouble spots by asking questions. This trains the writer to look and analyze, which helps develop independence in the writer.

---

6   **coach**: This term is used here to refer to anyone providing feedback that includes responsibility for helping the student improve his or her writing. It's more than just comments but less than direct instruction.

Here are a few examples of good coaching on pieces of writing.

- Coach reads the piece, recognizing areas that could be improved. Viewing the piece overall and its strengths and weaknesses, the coach decides the writer most needs to improve the logical flow of paragraphs. The overall communication is acknowledged, and questions then direct the writer's attention to this one area needing work.

- Coach reads student's piece, noting that ideas don't tie together well, the conclusion is weak, tenses are often inconsistent, and there are some spelling and punctuation errors. Despite all that, the writer makes a brilliant observation in the paper. The coach's feedback starts off: "You have so much to say here. I learned a lot! Hopefully, the places I've noted questions will help you find ways to say it even better." The coach then chooses the point most likely to create the most improvement, or the main point the student is known to be working on.

- Coach reads a well-written paper that shows, in the coach's view, better writing skills than the coach has, though there is one area of suggestion. Coach: "Wow. I thought this was really well written and to the point. It was interesting and informative from start to end! One thing that might be helpful: Did you intend to start so many sentences with *therefore*? Halfway through the paper, I realized I was being distracted by that a little. Anyway, for more useful feedback or coaching, you need a more skilled writer than me because I think it's all great!"

There will be times when you have to finalize a piece of writing without any feedback, especially in educational settings, and particularly for any type of examination. What do you do? Provide your own feedback! Set the piece aside and pick it up later or just keep a fresh viewpoint as you revise and refine.

*With practice, you can learn to provide
your own best feedback.*

STEP SEVEN: FINISH THE PIECE

The final step with a piece of writing is to finish it. But what is meant by "finishing" a piece of writing?

Normally, *finish* simply means to bring to an end. But as an experienced artist, artisan[7], technician[8] or skilled worker of any kind, one instinctively knows the difference between *ending* something and *finishing* something.

Consider two house painters. House painter Bob paints the outside of a house. When he's done, he ends the job and leaves. There are some empty cans, used brushes and spilled paint. There is tape still hanging from the eaves. There are a few spots that were missed. But he ended the job, didn't he?

House painter Joe, on the other hand, paints the outside of a house. He then *finishes* the job. He ensures it looks great, that it's fully done, and he cleans everything up, leaving no mess or undone work. That's *finishing* the job.

As a writer, you are learning skills that you use to make finished pieces. Whether you think of yourself as an artist, an artisan, a technician or just a skilled worker, it will help to know the difference between *ending* a piece and *finishing* a piece.

Just as the homeowner appreciates house painter Joe, so will your readers appreciate you!

So, how do you finish a piece? You need to know what your own standard is for a finished piece of writing, and then meet that standard!

---

7 **artisan**: someone who applies special skills in making things, particularly by hand, such as those who make ceramic dishes, leather goods, jewelry, clothing, furniture, etc.
8 **technician**: someone skilled in servicing or repairing machines, such as computers, automobiles, electronic equipment, etc.

PART 1 THE SEVEN STEPS

If it's an email to a friend, know your standard and meet it.

If it's a critique of a literature book, know your standard and meet it.

If it's an application for your dream college or dream job, know your standard and meet it.

Read the piece as if you've never read it before and ask:

1. Does it accomplish its purpose?
2. Does it speak to your audience?
3. Is it well organized?
4. Was it built from a strong first draft?
5. Did you revise and refine it enough?
6. Did you incorporate useful feedback (even if only your own)?
7. Did you *finish* it?

You may have already realized this, but part of finishing a piece concerns the subject of proofreading.

If Bob and Joe were writers instead of house painters, Bob would be the one who never proofreads his written work, or at best does it poorly. Joe is the one who proofreads the piece thoroughly as his final step.

The term *proofreading* comes from the fields of printing and publishing.[9] And if you think of your piece being ready for printing in a magazine or book, you'll get the idea.

---

9 Before computers and modern printers and copiers, written works were prepared for printing by putting every single letter in place in a block, covering the letters with ink, and then pressing paper to it—for every page. The first print was called a *proof*, a term still used for the first print of something that is then reviewed to make sure it looks exactly as intended. Thus, *proofreading* means reading the proof, finding any missed errors and correcting them, after which one prints the piece in its final, finished form.

PART 1 THE SEVEN STEPS

If the standard you are trying to meet is high, the proofreading standard needs to be high as well. The goal is not perfection. The goal is clear, effective communication.

But keep in mind Bob and Joe. One is a real professional. The other— not so much.

A few tips on proofreading you may wish to try for yourself:

- Read it aloud, slowly, paying close attention to what's actually on the page.
- Set it aside, then after a bit of time, read it newly.
- Look through the piece for those things you tend to miss or have trouble with.

If you think you have trouble proofreading, don't conclude that you're not a good proofreader. As with anything else, if you work at it, you will improve.

Eventually, you will be confident of your ability to finish a piece of writing and know that it is truly *finished*!

Setting your standard high for every finished piece of writing is the best way to become a skilled writer.

Part 2

THE PARTS

This section describes and discusses the parts of every piece of nonfiction writing: words, sentences, paragraphs and sections. If you know the parts and understand what they do, you will be able to put them together effectively.

WORDS

The most basic component[1] of your written communication is *words*. Your *ideas* will only arrive in the reader's mind to the degree that you can accurately translate them into *words* on the page. To help you with this, here are seven tips on using words well.

1. **Don't use words you aren't certain of.**

   It might surprise you how often a writer uses a word he or she doesn't fully understand, but it happens. In research papers and similar assignments, students can be found writing words they have read or heard but failed to fully understand. This can give the reader an inexplicable "foggy" feeling. There's no shame in ensuring you *understand* the words you are using before you use them; experienced writers do it all the time.

2. **Try to use words your reader will understand.**

   It's generally wise to use words the reader will understand without long explanations or frequent trips to the dictionary. You don't have to limit your vocabulary unnecessarily, just think of the reader in choosing words.

3. **Don't over-explain unfamiliar words.**

   On the other hand, when a writer starts explaining every word that might be unfamiliar to readers, it interrupts the flow of ideas. Excessive explanations can also come across as condescending, making the reader think: "Does this writer think I'm stupid?" (The footnoted word on this page might be an example of this for you if you already fully understood the word *component*!)

---

1 **component**: a part of a whole; one of the parts something is made of. For example, one of the *components* of a successful business is good promotion, or the *components* of water are hydrogen and oxygen. The word comes from *com-* "together" + *ponere* "to put." All components put together make up the whole.

PART 2 THE PARTS

4. **Avoid using fancy words that aren't necessary.**

   Resist any urge to appear smart or clever by using large or fancy words you don't need. Your goal is effective communication, not impressing your reader.

5. **Avoid using informal language.**

   Use language appropriate to the audience and purpose of the piece. Words used informally with friends or family are often inappropriate in professional speaking or writing. If you're unsure, check a dictionary or other resource.

6. **Avoid overusing a word.**

   Repeating the same word too often or too near an earlier use of that word can make the writing monotonous. For example, *The visitors enjoyed visiting all the city museums* sounds better as *The visitors enjoyed exploring all the city museums*. Even in the same paragraph, a noun or adjective used more than once or twice can be repetitive. Vary words to maintain interest.

7. **Eliminate unnecessary words.**

   Unnecessary words interfere with the clarity or flow of a sentence, making your message harder to receive. With practice, you can become skilled in spotting them, but here are some examples to help you get started.

   - Unneeded prepositions:

write up that report	*write that report*
took his hands off of the book	*took his hands off the book*

   - Unneeded describing words:

the stars sparkled brightly	*the stars sparkled*
The incredibly sweet, caramel ice cream was going down her chin impossibly fast.	*The caramel ice cream poured down her chin.*

- Words that repeat something already stated or obvious:

Basketball is a sport that is played all over the world.	*Basketball is played all over the world.*
He is a man who loves good cooking.	*He loves good cooking.*

- Wordy phrases:

Snow is falling at the present time.	*It's snowing.*
The fact that we have won three championships only motivates us to be a better team.	*Three championships only motivate us to be better.*
Findings from surveys made it apparent that we needed to update our advertising efforts to align them with the styles and trends of young adults today.	*Surveys showed the need to tailor our advertising to young adults.*

Other than tip #1, which should be followed strictly, all these tips require some judgment. They are not given here as firm rules, but as helpful advice. The goal is to get your message across as simply and clearly as possible.

Practice using these tips, and your writing will gradually become simpler, clearer and easier to read.

SENTENCES

There are countless ways to put words together into sentences, but some are more effective than others. This chapter provides some basics, tips and suggestions on sentence writing.

What Is a Sentence?

A **sentence** is a group of words that has a subject and its verb, and it expresses a complete thought. It can be simple or complicated, short or long. It can have multiple subjects, verbs and descriptive phrases.

The following sentences are composed differently, but they all communicate a complete thought.

She reads.

The boy loves playing competitive basketball.

Run! (with the understood subject "you")

After it rains in the country, the air is fragrant with the scents of grass and flowers and trees.

The children desperately wanted to see the cougar that had been seen in the forest the previous week, so they found a spot at the edge of the trees and, with their picnic lunch and blanket, sat and ate and spoke in whispers, and watched all afternoon—not surprisingly, in vain.

There are two main groups of words that are most often mistaken for sentences: the sentence fragment and the run-on sentence.

PART 2 THE PARTS

The Sentence Fragment

A **fragment** is a small piece of something. A **sentence fragment** is a piece of a sentence used as a sentence. It is *not* a complete sentence because it lacks a subject or its verb, or it does not express a complete thought. Each of the following is a sentence fragment:

> *The falling snow.*
>
> *In the evening.*
>
> *Feeling exhilarated by the win!*
>
> *While she was writing her first novel.*
>
> *Depending on whether or not you want to finish your work today or tomorrow.*

None of these are complete thoughts. They've been written with ending punctuation marks here to show how a sentence fragment is written *as if it were* a sentence; however, putting an ending punctuation mark at the end of an incomplete thought does not make it a sentence.

You can correct these by adding the missing subject or verb or other needed words to make it a complete thought.

> *The falling snow was beautiful.*
>
> *They took a walk in the evening.*
>
> *She was feeling exhilarated by the win!*
>
> *While she was writing her first novel, she traveled throughout western Europe.*
>
> *Depending on whether or not you want to finish your work today or tomorrow, you can do it now or put it off.*

PART 2 THE PARTS

Once you understand and can easily recognize accidental use of sentence fragments, you may on occasion *decide* to use a sentence fragment for effect. Here's an example.

Ah, the sun! I had waited all winter to enjoy its warmth again.

You can see the difference between this usage and the earlier examples of sentence fragments—this one is clearly used for a specific effect.

The Run-On Sentence

A **run-on sentence** is two or more complete sentences put together without a conjunction or correct punctuation. Here is an example:

Jaden went to every soccer game, the team was winning them all!

The most common ways to correct a run-on sentence are these:

- Separate the sentences with a period.

    Jaden went to every soccer game. The team was winning them all!

- If the sentences are closely related, you can separate them with a semicolon.

    Jaden went to every soccer game; the team was winning them all!

- Join the sentences with a conjunction.

    Jaden went to every soccer game, and the team was winning them all!

    Jaden went to every soccer game because the team was winning them all!

It should be noted that connecting two very short sentences with a comma can be acceptable. Here are a couple examples:

People talk, animals listen.

Leave yesterday, live today.

PART 2 THE PARTS

Sentence Rhythm and Variety

Rhythm is the regular recurrence of something, a pattern that repeats in a way that the observer, listener or audience can recognize it. People enjoy experiencing rhythm, especially if it's not so repetitive that it becomes boring.

Here are some examples of rhythm:

>short, short, long
>>short, short, long
>>>short, short, long

>red, blue, red, red, blue
>>red, blue, red, red, blue
>>>red, blue, red, red, blue

>STRONG, STRONG, weak.
>>STRONG, STRONG, weak.
>>>STRONG, STRONG, weak.
>>>>STRONG, STRONG, weak.
>>>>>STRONG, STRONG, weak.

You might have noticed with this last example that it started to get boring. It was due for some change, or variety, to maintain interest.

Rhythm in writing can be created in different ways. Here's a simple example:

>*She loved the spring garden—the sprouting plants, the fresh flowers, the baby birds.*

Can you see and hear the rhythm? Here's another example:

>*Love music? Love dancing? Love games? Come to the "70s Disco Night" Saturday 8pm-midnight!*

Here's a different example:

> *Walking down the alley, Briana was suddenly startled by a barking dog. Terrified, she froze. Should she shout? Should she run? Should she cry for help? Or should she try to be friendly? As the dog approached her, she was about to scream when she noticed what she had failed to notice before: a wagging tail and a friendly dog who was happy to see someone he knew. Her fear turned to relief as she recognized her friend's dog, Farley.*

In this paragraph you can probably notice both repeated patterns *and* variety. They help make the writing interesting to read.

By contrast, here's a paragraph with only short, choppy sentences:

> *Danielle walked to school. She picked some flowers. She wove the flowers into a bracelet. She arrived to school late.*

Here's a paragraph with longer sentences, but again, without variety:

> *When he decided to apply to Michigan State, he knew he needed to fill out the application forms. After filling out the forms, there would be letters of recommendation to get. Along with these letters, he would have to write two different essays about himself. Additionally, he would have to talk to his parents about helping him with the finances.*

Both of these examples show how a rhythm can get boring if the writer uses the same kind of sentence again and again.

There are many ways to create rhythm and variety. As you continue to write, and as you continue to read writing you enjoy, stop to notice how the writer uses both rhythm and variety.

PART 2 THE PARTS

The Power of Brevity[2]

Concise writing has impact.

Additionally, the time you invest in trimming will normally pay off in improved clarity and simplicity—and happier readers.

While developing your own style, don't be afraid of simple thoughts and simple sentences. When you know what you want to say, it can usually be said simply. Should all sentences be short? No. But by eliminating unneeded words, you will find your writing becoming stronger and more powerful.

Sentences of Different Importance

You may not have considered it, but not all sentences are equally important.

For instance, you may have a specific idea that you want to stick with the reader—everything else is intended to set up that one sentence which has unique importance.

With a sentence that you want to have extra power or impact, be willing to give it more time and attention.

Important Sentences or Words Placed Last

An important sentence can lead off a piece or a section; however, placing a sentence last in a paragraph or section will give it more impact.

The same is true with the placement of words in sentences. Compare the following:

> *Charles stumbled into an angry bobcat while exploring the crawl space under his house!*

> *While exploring the crawl space under his house, Charles stumbled into an angry bobcat!*

Both sentences are fine, but the second one has a bit more "punch."

---

2 **brevity**: the quality of being brief, short, concise; in speech or writing, it means using just the words needed, no more.

PART 2 THE PARTS

The Beauty of a Great Sentence

The preceding comments and tips can help you write more effective sentences. To further this, what follows are four short excerpts of nonfiction by well-known writers.

You may find one or more of them challenging. You may or may not find them inspiring or particularly useful to you as a young writer. Nevertheless, they show a range of different types of sentences as crafted by skilled writers.

> *These are the times that try men's souls. The summer soldier and the sunshine patriot will, in this crisis, shrink from the service of their country; but he that stands by it now, deserves the love and thanks of man and woman. Tyranny, like hell, is not easily conquered; yet we have this consolation with us, that the harder the conflict, the more glorious the triumph. What we obtain too cheap, we esteem too lightly: it is dearness only that gives everything its value. Heaven knows how to put a proper price upon its goods; and it would be strange indeed if so celestial an article as FREEDOM should not be highly rated.*
>
> From *The Crisis*
> Thomas Paine 1776

> *In those early days I had already published one little thing ('The Jumping Frog') in an Eastern paper, but I did not consider that that counted. In my view, a person who published things in a mere newspaper could not properly claim recognition as a Literary Person: he must rise away above that; also, he must appear in a magazine. He would then be a Literary Person; also, he would be famous—right away. These two ambitions were strong upon me. This was in 1866. I prepared my contribution, and then looked around for the best magazine to go up to glory in.*
>
> From *My Debut as a Literary Person*
> Mark Twain c. 1870

PART 2 THE PARTS

Some have God's words; others have songs of comfort for the bereaved. If I can pluck up the courage here, I would like to speak directly to the dead—the September dead.

From "The Dead of September 11"
Toni Morrison 2001

For some weeks now I have been engaged in dispersing the contents of this apartment, trying to persuade hundreds of inanimate objects to scatter and leave me alone. It is not a simple matter. I am impressed by the reluctance of one's worldly goods to go out again into the world.

From "Good-bye to Forty-Eighth Street"
E.B. White 1957

PARAGRAPHS

A **paragraph** is normally defined as a group of sentences that addresses one main idea, but occasionally a paragraph is a single sentence. Regardless of length, paragraphs are the main building blocks of pieces of writing.

Paragraph Length

Longer paragraphs tend to create a slower, more methodical pace. Shorter paragraphs help speed the reader along.

A short paragraph can also be used among longer paragraphs for increased impact or emphasis. Here's an example:

> It was a blustery, fall day when I jogged to the stable to exercise my friend's horse, Charley. He towered over me as I led him to the fenced field for a workout. Soon he began prancing, happy to be out in the sun. I could feel his excitement growing, so I tightened my grip on his halter in the hope that we would arrive at the paddock together.
>
> That hope was in vain.
>
> As a gust threw rousing scents into his nostrils, Charley reared, broke free, and left me face down in the dust.

Though a long paragraph can be useful when you have a lot to say on one main idea, be aware that a long paragraph can look like an impassable wall of text. Consider breaking it down into smaller sub-ideas that each have their own paragraph. This can help speed your reader along.

Generally speaking, longer paragraphs work for more formal pieces and for more literate audiences.

PART 2 THE PARTS

Paragraph Integrity[3]

Think of paragraphs as individual stepping stones on the path you want your reader to follow. Here are a few tips to help you make each step a sure one:

- Try to stick to one main idea for each paragraph.
- Make each paragraph easy to read by making each sentence within the paragraph flow smoothly one to the next.
- Within a paragraph, don't contradict the main idea. If you want to present a contradicting view, put it in another paragraph.

Paragraph Continuity

To make a path of stepping stones easy to walk, you space the stones so a person doesn't have to "jump" from one to another. Do the same with your paragraphs by making the flow between paragraphs smooth and logical. The ideas shouldn't be "far apart," requiring the reader to "jump" too far. Notice how one paragraph leads into the next in this excerpt from *Getting Your Point Across in Writing* (Heron Books, 2019):

> This last point can be a hidden barrier to good writing: the person thinks their own ideas aren't interesting enough, good enough or important enough to share.
>
> This sort of thinking is probably the biggest reason for every failure that ever happened in the history of the world! Someone thought their ideas weren't interesting enough, good enough or important enough to communicate.
>
> It's not a very good excuse.
>
> You have your ideas. Don't be afraid to share them. The worst that can happen is someone will disagree with you. Great! Maybe you'll end up learning something. Maybe you'll succeed in getting the other person to reexamine their own ideas. Maybe both of these

---

3 **integrity**: the quality of being complete or whole as itself, without missing or unnecessary parts.

things will happen. Whatever happens, your communication can be the first step toward changing the way things are.

In conclusion:

Leading a reader smoothly to your intended destination requires paragraphs that are composed and connected well.

SECTIONS

Unless a piece of nonfiction writing is short, it will have sections or parts made up of several paragraphs each. They might not be called "sections" or labeled in any way, but they are how the piece is built.

If paragraphs can be thought of as stepping stones, sections can be thought of as signposts that orient your reader to changes in direction or to major portions of the path, like chapters of a book.

Though a piece can be organized in many ways, the simplest structure is usually thought of this way:

> introduction (or *lead*)
>
> body (or *story*)
>
> conclusion (or *close*)

Introduction (or lead)

Every piece has some sort of introduction, a way to bring the reader smoothly into the topic.

In reporting for news, magazines, or online articles, this opening is often thought of as the *lead*, because it leads, or comes first. You can also think of it as how you get the reader's interest and lead them into the piece; thus, the idea of starting with a *lead* can be applied to any nonfiction writing.

PART 2 THE PARTS

There are many ways to write a lead, but here are some that have proven effective:

- Use a quote from an outside source that relates to the message you want to communicate.

   John Rainer, noted biologist and researcher, said in an exclusive interview with the editor of "A New Day," May 1996, "Each year billions of leaves go to waste when they could be quenching the thirst of countless numbers of Americans."

- Use a remarkable or startling fact or a surprising statistic relating to your message.

   Each year, Americans have had to cut back on the amount of water they use per day. Last year, each family was allowed to use eighty gallons a day. This year the allowed use was reduced to seventy gallons.

- Use a rhetorical question to introduce your point.
  (A **rhetorical question** is a question asked to produce an effect, not to gather information, such as "Who can tell whether or not life exists on Jupiter?")

   Is the number one question on everyone's mind these days the high cost of building a spaceship? No. The number one concern of every American is the dwindling supply of clean water.

- Use an anecdote to introduce your message.
  (An **anecdote** is an interesting, sometimes amusing, short story about a real incident or person.)

   Sally ran excitedly into the house carrying a large basket of eggs she had just gathered. She gently placed the basket on the kitchen table and went to the sink to get a drink of water. When she turned on the faucet and nothing came out, she began to wonder if we had finally run out of water or if this was just a warning of things to come.

- Use a personal experience that relates to your point.

> *Until I read Jack Stem's article "They Aren't Just Leaves," I never paid too much attention to leaves except to admire the array of blues, greens and pinks in the spring and the shades of reds, oranges and yellows in the fall.*

However you choose to start a piece of writing, keep in mind that a good introduction or lead will pull your audience into the topic and launch them on the path you intend to take them down.

Body (or story)

The body will comprise the majority of the piece.

It will take the reader through a sequence of ideas that make your overall point or deliver your overall message. It's a well-organized path to your intended destination.

In reporting or providing a narrative[4], it will tell a story, taking the reader through a sequence of events, painting the picture you want to create.

Most of your organizational planning for a major piece will involve working out what the body, or story, will consist of and how it will be best sequenced.

Conclusion (or close)

The conclusion is where you bring your reader to the final destination, arrive to the overall message or point, and effectively *close* the piece of writing.

When useful, it can summarize major points, reminding the reader how the conclusion was arrived at. It should not, however, just repeat things already said. It should conclude them, wrap them up.

---

4 **narrative:** any account of a sequence of events, like a story; from Latin *narrativus,* "telling a story."

PART 2 THE PARTS

If your piece is designed to engage the reader into thought or action, this is where that should happen, leaving them with something to think about or do as a result of your message. For example, if your piece is a formal proposal, this is where your solution or plan of action is finally presented in a concise way.

The trick with a good conclusion is ending the adventure smoothly. Too long a conclusion can cause disinterest or annoyance in the reader. Too abrupt a conclusion will make the reader feel they've been dropped off a cliff.

> *A well-organized piece draws readers in, orients them, takes them on a journey, and wraps things up smoothly.*

Part 3

THE TYPES

This section explains common types of nonfiction writing: persuasive, personal, business and academic.

PERSUASIVE

To **persuade** someone is to say things that will get them to agree with a certain view or take a certain action. Persuasive writing has many uses:

- Essay[1] writing—Most often, when writing an essay for schoolwork or for publication, you are trying to persuade the reader that a certain view or opinion is correct.
- Proposals—Any written proposal is intended to persuade or convince someone that a certain action is the correct one.
- Political action—A letter or email to a politician, or a speech written for political purposes, is normally persuasive.

To be effective, you should start any persuasive piece with a statement of the opinion being proposed or the problem being addressed.

Creating Your Thesis

In school, whether high school or college, the term **thesis** is normally used when talking about the point of a persuasive essay. It is defined as the main point or opinion in a written assignment, normally introduced at or near the beginning.

It is assumed that a thesis is worth writing about, that it is a specific and independent idea requiring some persuasion. For example, *many people use social media* wouldn't work well as a thesis; it's not an independent idea and requires no persuasion because everyone agrees with it already. On the other hand, *young people need increased guidance on the safe and productive use of social media* could work as a thesis. It's not something everyone would immediately agree with and requires explanation and persuasion.

---

1 **essay**: a short piece of writing on a subject, usually presenting the writer's personal views.

PART 3 THE TYPES

Even if you are responding to a specific question, taking time to develop a thesis will help focus your thoughts and writing. Here are some tips to do this.

- **Learn about the subject**
  In the above example, the subject is *use of social media*.

- **Narrow to a specific issue**
  Who uses social media to what effect? Business professionals, especially in sales and marketing. Politicians to affect public opinion. Teens, for good or ill.

- **Ask questions**
  What are the bad effects of social media for teens? The good effects? How does one intelligently weigh the good and bad effects? Can the good effects be strengthened and the bad effects minimized? If so, how? Instruction, advice? What kind? How provided? Teachers? Parents? Opinion leaders? Such questions help guide further research, observation or thought.

- **Develop a definite opinion, argument or proposal**
  There are ways to minimize the bad effects and maximize the good effects of social media. Since virtually all teens use social media, they should all have the opportunity to learn about them. Again, this can help focus further research, observation or thought on the topic.

- **Refine the thesis**
  You want a statement of opinion, argument or proposal that requires some persuasion. This means your thesis isn't obviously true and is something you can reasonably defend. *Young people need increased guidance on the safe and productive use of social media, not restriction from its use.* This isn't obviously true and it can be defended.

These simple steps can be used to develop a workable thesis, after which you will be able to begin organizing the piece.

PART 3 THE TYPES

Developing Your Argument

One way to think of and describe what you are doing in a persuasive piece of writing is you are making an argument. In persuasive writing, an **argument** is not people voicing disagreement with each other. It means the set of reasons that support your opinion, point or proposal.

In making a proposal or stating a definite opinion, you will have things that agree with your point and things that don't agree with your point. These are often called the **pros** and **cons**.[2]

> *pros: points that agree with and support the thesis*
>
> *cons: points that disagree with and refute[3] the thesis*

In developing your argument, it can be effective to start with the cons. By first openly and honestly presenting opposing views, it shows you are not afraid of them or avoiding them. You can then walk your reader through the pros and find they are now more compelling. Here are some cons for the sample thesis regarding the guidance of youth using social media:

> *Young people often reject advice from adults on the use of social media. They feel that older people don't understand modern life the way they do and just want to restrict them. Additionally, technology is changing so rapidly, today's advice can quickly become outdated.*
>
> *One must also recognize that teens have needs they often feel aren't understood by adults. What happens on social media can represent an important part of this private world of a teen—private from the prying eyes and opinions about "safety" that adults want to provide. Besides, experience—not advice—is usually the better teacher, isn't it?*

---

2 The term *argument* can also be used to refer to one of the points supporting your thesis, instead of the whole set of points. The term *counterargument* can be used for any point opposing your thesis. Thus, pros and cons are sometimes called arguments and counterarguments.

3 **refute**: say that some statement or idea is not correct or not true.

PART 3 THE TYPES

Assuming you've provided your thesis statement at the beginning of the piece, the reader can see right away that you have given honest consideration to opposing views.

In presenting cons, look at the topic from different viewpoints. Try to anticipate beliefs or attitudes your reader or readers may have that will prevent them from accepting your thesis. Continuing our example, here are further cons that consider an important counterargument:

> *Research has repeatedly shown that many teens experience tremendous negativity from social media: intimidation, jealousy, self-worth issues, unrealistic expectations—in short, more sadness than joy. And this says nothing of its addictive nature, which can result in a much less "social" existence in the real world of physical, expressive, face-to-face interaction.*
>
> *As absurd as it may sound, might we not all be better off removing social media from our lives altogether? Don't laugh. Increasing numbers of social media addicts, including well-known influencers, are swearing off their social networking apps after noticing the short- and long-term negative effects on themselves and others.*

By first presenting counterarguments, you provide a foundation upon which you can build your supporting points. If you find your pros don't address all the cons, it can help you see holes in your research or thinking. Though not in the exact sequence given, the following shows the various example cons all being addressed, transitioning smoothly from the last paragraph above.

> *The realities of modern life, however, demand a more thoughtful view of social media, including its power for good in the hands of young people.*
>
> *Yes, teens may often experience emotional struggles, but hasn't this been true for decades, from the days long before social media?*
>
> *Yes, social media addiction is a problem, but is it factually more of a problem for teens than adults? Television addicts weren't*

PART 3 THE TYPES

> *cured by eliminating TVs from the world any more than alcohol addiction was resolved by Prohibition.*
>
> *And the argument that teens won't listen to adults is not a new one. Fifty years ago, it was called "the generation gap." But whatever label is assigned to a breakdown in communication, nothing changes a parent's basic role in helping prepare children for successful adulthood.*
>
> *Then and now, it is a parent's role to foster a healthy relationship with their child, providing love and understanding, support and advice. Any young person feeling severe emotional stress, struggling with addiction, or feeling their parents just "don't understand," is a young person needing adult attention and communication, not blanket restriction from interaction on social media.*

Having addressed the cons, one can then move on to the main pros one has been leading up to. Again, what follows transitions smoothly from the preceding paragraph:

> *After all, social media is just that: media. It's a way, a path, for communication. Understanding its proper and improper uses is part of learning to live successfully in today's world. As in all matters of a personal or social nature, parents play a primary role in guiding their children in its use. And other adults can often provide meaningful assistance.*
>
> *Nor can one ignore the positive potentials of social media and the value of young people being familiar with its use. As just one example, in oppressive or dangerous environments, social media allows for fast communication and coordination—not only powerful in helping effect change but, sometimes, saving lives.*

PART 3 THE TYPES

Crafting Your Conclusion

Make your conclusion count by tying it together with your thesis and argument and encouraging the reader to take some action or consider a change of heart.

> *Today's world may be more complex, with even greater challenges facing both young people and adults. The answers lie in more and better communication, not more and harsher restrictions. Let's use the lessons learned over many generations, lessons that encourage helping young people succeed in the world in which they live and will soon lead. By identifying and sharing sound guidance, advice and care, we can all improve the safe and productive use of social media, not only for our youth, but for all of us.*

Persuasive writing should take your reader from the thesis through the pros and cons to a clear, logical, concise conclusion.

Summary

Not all persuasive writing will be as lengthy or detailed as this example may appear, but the basic approach can be the same.

> *Narrow down the main point you want to make, show a balanced approach to your reasoning, and bring it all together in a strong conclusion.*

PERSONAL

Whether you consider it easy or hard, there will be times when you need to write about yourself—we'll call it *personal writing*. Though you may think doing so is quite a bit different than other nonfiction writing, it's not.

The most common uses of personal writing will be these:

- personal letters, whether by post or email, including announcements, invitations and thank you letters[4]
- blogs detailing trips, adventures, projects, etc.
- applications for schools or employment
- school assignments which ask for, or work well with, personal stories, anecdotes, descriptions or experiences

How formal you need to be will depend on circumstances. When in doubt, lean toward formality rather than risk rejection due to a style that is too informal.

If there's one key piece of advice on personal writing, it's this: In writing about yourself, don't ramble, even if it's a narrative. Your reader will appreciate if you write as if you were showing them a good photograph, or two or three, not a long, drawn-out movie. If you can "write" a good picture or two, you're probably on the right track. This means focusing on one or two key things, and rather than explaining them, painting a picture with plenty of details.

> *If advices on nonfiction writing seem hard to apply to personal writing, it's a sure sign to focus on them even more.*

---

[4] A sample letter and addressed envelope are given in the reference section at the back of the book.

BUSINESS

For business and professional applications, it is best to be concise. State why you are writing, make your point efficiently with adequate specifics, and conclude with your proposal, offer or what you want to accomplish. The busier or more important the recipient, the harder you should work to achieve brevity.

Proposals

In the professional world, many good ideas never see the light of day simply because the ability to write a good proposal is missing. It goes like this:

Great idea + weak (or no) proposal = no action

Weak idea + great proposal = wasted action

Great idea + great proposal = successful action

A proposal should include these elements:

1. A simple, clear introduction.
2. A clean statement of the situation, problem or opportunity being addressed.
3. Information (facts) needed to understand the proposed solution.
4. Personnel, financial and deadline considerations as appropriate.
5. The conclusion—what you are proposing to handle the situation or problem or to take advantage of the opportunity.

Good proposals bridge the gap from idea to action. Even a successful verbal proposal will often need to be backed up by a written version that others will need to be able to read, understand and sign off on.

PART 3 THE TYPES

Résumés

A **résumé** is a summary of educational, professional and other work experience qualifications for a job.[5] It can be accompanied by a brief cover letter requesting an interview.

Even though it often contains the same information included in a job application, a résumé should sell that you are a well-qualified applicant. While a good résumé shows your qualifications for the job, a cover letter can communicate how you may be an especially good fit for the job and group.

Additionally, one résumé may not work for all positions or groups, so you may need to create more than one. Recruiters are more likely to read an original résumé targeting the specific position they are trying to fill.

Many samples and templates can be found online. Here are a few simple tips:

- Ideally, it's a single page, organized well and easy to look at and read.

- It should show a progression of education and work history clearly, including dates, with no unexplained time gaps—most recent first and progressing backward in time.

- It should show actions and accomplishments, not just positions. For example, "Supervised sales team to 30% increase in net profits over previous year." (Sounds more professional than "I supervised....")

- Include skills that would serve the group to which you are reaching out, but only if they are notable and worth mentioning. For example, the ability to speak Spanish or Chinese might be very valuable in certain situations or fluency with graphic design or web development software.

---

[5] A CV or Curriculum Vitae (Latin for "course of life") is a similar, longer summary of experience with emphasis on academic achievements and degrees, commonly used when applying for higher academic or research opportunities or positions. Sometimes the terms *résumé* and *CV* are used interchangeably.

- Try to paint a picture of your growth as an individual.

Above all, be simple, honest and factual, and speak to the person and group to which you are seeking employment.

Expository Business Letters

An expository[6] business letter explains a request or a need. Write this sort of business letter to order merchandise or services, or to request information of a business.

There are many different requests or demands to make in life. It could be as simple as reversing a charge on your credit card for something you returned, or as complex as a letter seeking fair treatment in a legal matter.

Even if you never work in a business, there will arise situations in which you need to write expository business letters or emails just to take care of the business of life.[7]

> *The ability to write concisely and professionally is often a direct index of how far an individual can rise, regardless of profession.*

---

6 **expository**: that "exposes," explains or describes something, that brings it into open view.

7 A sample business letter in commonly used format can be found in the reference section at the back of the book.

ACADEMIC

This chapter gives advice specific to the kinds of nonfiction assignments that are commonly required in school, though the skills developed in academic writing will be found to have applications far beyond the classroom.[8]

Persuasive Essays

Covered thoroughly in an earlier chapter, persuasive writing is commonly expected in school, particularly where the instructor wants to see what *you* think.

A good educational program or teacher will demand much persuasive writing of you, as it helps evaluate information for yourself, not simply repeat back what you've read.

Though such an assignment may be focused on your interpretation, your thoughts, or your conclusions regarding some area of study, it's good to think of it as demanding you be *persuasive*. This will encourage you to back up your ideas, rather than just state them, to persuade your reader toward your view or conclusion. Even if the assignment is short, the principles covered earlier of thesis, pros and cons, and conclusion will prove useful to successful persuasive writing.

Expository or Descriptive Reports

Expository writing explains by providing information. It differs from persuasive writing in that its purpose is to give facts and information, not to express an opinion. A "report" is normally expository. An "essay" is normally persuasive.

---

[8] Information on common-format standards for academic writing are given in the reference section at the back of the book.

PART 3 THE TYPES

Here are examples of assignments where the writing would be expository:

- A summary of what occurred in an exercise, for example: "Using what you've learned about surveys, talk to five different people about their favorite book; then write up your observations."
- A summary of a science experiment, including what exactly was done, what outcomes were expected, and what the actual results were.
- A report on the factors that led up to a historic event.
- An explanation of how some process or procedure is done.

Descriptive writing describes something in detail, such as a person, place, thing or event. A description of a person might tell what the person looks like, what their hopes and dreams are, or how they act. A description of a place often describes how things are arranged or perceived through the senses. An event is usually described as a sequence of actions.

Here are example assignments where descriptive writing is used:

- A book report that includes a description of the main character or a key event as part of it.
- A character sketch, where you "draw a picture" of someone you have studied about or someone you know well.
- A report on places visited on a trip.
- Any assignment that specifically asks for description.

These two types of writing are mentioned together here because they often overlap. Though creativity can come into play, in both expository and descriptive writing, you will mainly be sticking to the facts as you focus on reporting, explaining and describing.

PART 3 THE TYPES

Narrative Essays and Assignments

Narrate means "tell a story." Though we tend to think of "telling stories" as fiction writing, you can tell a nonfiction story as well. When you are recounting an event or sequence of events, it is a narrative piece.

In some ways, narrative essays allow for more creativity than other types. Examples can include these:

- biographical or autobiographical sketches
- use of an event or sequence of events to illustrate some lesson, precept or theme
- college application essays that expect a narrative approach

When writing a narrative essay, even though it is nonfiction, consider these elements of storytelling:

Narrator or storyteller. That's you. Though the use of *I* and *me* in formal writing is usually a sign of inexperience, narrative writing will often require it. You can also assume a viewpoint other than your own if it's part of the assignment or if it will make the narration more interesting.

Plot. A narrative essay needs some sort of plot, meaning a planned sequence of events that engages the reader and pulls them along. Realize it can be effective to start in the middle or most exciting or challenging part, then back up and tell how it was arrived at and resolved.

Characters. If the people, or animals, of your narrative are realistic and likable, they will carry your narrative forward. If your narrative lacks life, look at how well you've given life to the characters that play roles in it.

Challenge. Characters in stories face challenges or barriers they need to overcome, or they face conflict or problems they need to solve. Without challenge or barriers the reader can relate to, the narrative may fall flat.

Setting and scenes. Any good story creates realistic settings and scenes the reader can feel a part of. A good narrative essay does the same.

Climax or conclusion. Be sure your narrative essay has a climax or ending that makes the journey worthwhile to the reader.

Research Papers

Research can be defined as investigation into some part of life in order to make new observations and conclusions, or to find solutions to problems. It usually includes study of the observations and conclusions made by others. Its purpose is new discoveries, insights or answers, even if only new to oneself. There are two approaches.

Small to big. You gather lots of (small) information, analyze it for patterns, sort out conflicting data, follow information trails that look promising, and so on. Ultimately, you hope to reach a single (big) discovery or conclusion.

This is called *inductive reasoning.* It goes from specific to general, from the small facts or details to the big principle or conclusion.

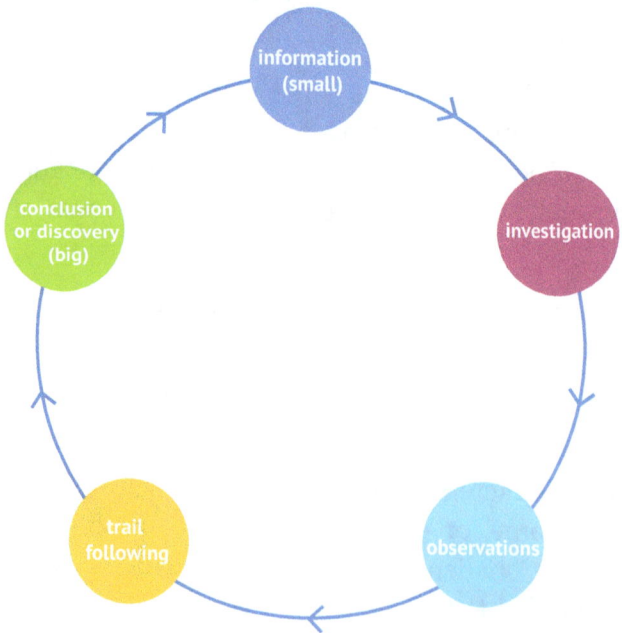

PART 3   THE TYPES

Big to small. You start with a (big) theory, conclusion or postulate[9], and then investigate the real world by testing to see if that idea works as shown in the (small) details of results.

This is called *deductive reasoning.* It goes from general to specific, from the big principle to the small facts that give evidence to its workability.

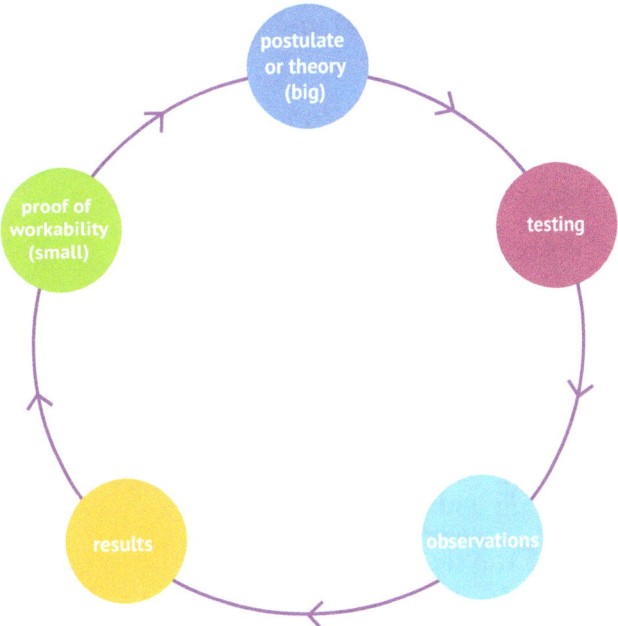

The circular pattern of these diagrams intends to show that one can continue where one started. In the first diagram, the conclusion can lead to further information and investigation. In the second, if the workability falls short, one can start with a new postulate and conduct further research.

One can, of course, combine these approaches. What's important is the purpose of the research: some new discovery, insight or solution.

Researching what car to buy can be used to illustrate the two approaches.

---

9   **postulate**: Something put forth as a truth to act as a starting point for investigation or discussion.

PART 3   THE TYPES

Small to big:

- You gather a lot of information, investigate various sources, make observations and follow up on things you read or hear, gradually narrowing the field.
- The pieces of information are small: makes, models, features, miles per gallon, prices new, prices used, size, appearance, comfort, etc.
- Eventually, you come to the conclusion that a used Toyota Corolla with 20,000 miles on it will best serve your needs, budget, insurance payments and so on.
- The conclusion is big: buy the used Corolla.

Big to small:

- Your father strongly suggests you purchase your uncle's small Chevy pickup truck. He says it's the right car at the right price at the right time—for you.
- You are starting with a big idea: the Chevy pickup is right.
- You test drive the truck, observing how well it drives, if everything works as it's supposed to, what kind of mileage it gets. You look at the results your uncle has gotten with it, how well it has held up. You look at what it would do to your budget to purchase it and keep it operating.
- Eventually, you come to the conclusion that it is a very workable plan and decide to make the purchase based on all the details of workability, which are small.

Experience in using each approach will help you recognize how and when it's appropriate to use them in combination; i.e., first learn each, then judgment will follow. Again, the overall importance is to achieve the purpose: in this case, *discovering* which car to buy.

Understanding these two approaches to investigation can be invaluable when it comes time to organize a research paper for school.

The purpose of research is to make new observations, conclusions, discoveries or insights. The purpose of a **research paper** is an accurate written report of the research done and the conclusions reached.

Whether your research took a big-to-small approach or a small-to-big approach, your research paper should walk the reader through the path of discovery. They should be able to understand what question or problem you started with, how you approached the research, where it led you, and what you discovered or concluded in the end.

Some teachers put great emphasis on the rules associated with research papers. This can include such absurdities as exactly how much space should be in each margin or a minimum number of notecards a student must write information on while researching! Though there can be valid educational reasons for rules a teacher might provide, overemphasis on things like format, instead of *research, writing* and *learning*, has discouraged many otherwise-interested students.

Again, the purpose of a research paper is to provide an accurate written report of the research done and what the results were. That's all.

It's actually very simple.

Done well, a research paper helps validate your work while increasing your certainty. It gives you a chance to review your path of reasoning and discovery, to double-check your logic, and to be sure about your results.

Also, more often than you might think, a good research paper teaches the reader something. Teachers love learning from students. The smartest teachers are smart, in part, because they're constantly learning from their students.

PART 3 THE TYPES

As long as we agree that research and research papers have valuable, sensible purposes, and that writing a research paper is actually simple, there are only a handful of things to watch for in doing research and writing about it.

1. Honesty

    The research has to be done honestly. You need to see things for yourself, evaluate information for yourself, and communicate honestly about whatever you discover. Don't pretend some observation or conclusion. Don't pretend some insight is yours if it's actually someone else's. Most importantly, don't sell yourself short[10]. Your ideas matter. Learn from others, yes, but be willing to explore your own ideas and insights. For some, this is a more challenging aspect to honesty in research.

2. Failing to actually *look*

    The easiest way to fall short in a research assignment is to do shallow research—in other words, fail to dig in and find the truth, or at least as close as you can get to it. The way to find useful data is to actually look and keep looking. You won't make any worthwhile discoveries if you take the first piece of information you find and decide that's all there is to know. Part of this is remaining unbiased, avoiding fixed ideas[11], spotting prejudices in your own thinking. And part of this is being willing to dig around, going beyond the first page of search results or the first few people interviewed. The answer is to actually *look* and *keep looking.*

---

10 **sell oneself short**: to undervalue oneself and one's abilities.

11 **fixed idea:** also referred to as *idée fixe* (French), a fixed idea is an obsession, some single idea that takes over one's mind and won't change. Normally used in psychology to describe a mental disorder, a fixed idea can also refer to any idea that is fixed, stuck, or won't change, even when faced with facts to the contrary. Any prejudice or bias is essentially a fixed idea.

3. Challenging illogic

    In any research, you will run across opposing views. Use your own ability to study and don't be afraid to challenge something that doesn't seem logical. Be willing to look at different viewpoints but remain alert for suspicious information. If you are studying a source (book, article, blog, website or direct interview) and they seem to align all information toward a particular agenda[12], use common sense and be wary of its validity.

4. Going earlier

    In researching, one of the best ways to get good information is to go as early as possible. Superficial research accepts an interpretation of an interpretation of an interpretation. You might be surprised how many people have confusions and misunderstandings but don't know it. The further you get from original sources, the greater your chance of getting faulty information. What was Michelangelo's purpose for creating the famous sculpture *David*? How does a particular professional athlete train for optimum performance? There may be many opinions or interpretations, but if you can find out what the person himself said, you will be more likely to have found true data. When researching, it's often useful to go earlier in order to get past the interpretations or opinions of others.

5. Keeping track of your path

    As you research, it is generally a good idea to keep some notes on where you are going, what you find, where you find it, and any early questions or possible conclusions you surface along the way. It will help you keep track of where you've been and where you're going, and it will help when it comes time to bring it all together in a paper, including citing[13] sources.

---

12 **agenda**: (informal) hidden or underlying intentions or objectives of a person or group.

13 **cite**: to quote or refer to information from someone else, particularly when it assists some point or argument you are trying to make. It comes from a Latin word meaning "to call upon." **Citation** refers to a single instance of citing a source.

PART 3   THE TYPES

6. Remaining objective

   A common error in research writing at the high school level is when the student walks the reader through the path of discovery as if it's a narrative essay about oneself: "I started my research by asking the question.... After I looked into... I then began to think...." Instead, be objective. "Should we move from gasoline-powered vehicles entirely? Pollution statistics show that.... Currently, less than 2% of passenger vehicles in the U.S. are fully electric." Most formal writing avoids the use of "I" altogether. Eliminate the first person pronouns (*I, me, we* and *us*) and notice the difference.

7. Opening the doors to knowledge

   Research papers typically require the citing of sources, also called *documentation.* This means providing reference to documents that support your information or opinions, or saying where you got a fact, opinion or idea. This allows the reader to explore that information or source further if interested, or to verify the accuracy of your statement or interpretation. Any time you are basing a line of reasoning on information that isn't common knowledge[14], you should make it easy for the reader to see where it's coming from. If you use someone else's words, use quotes and say who and where it came from. If you've restated someone else's ideas, you obviously wouldn't use quotes, but you would still make it clear where the ideas came from. Most plagiarism[15] in academic work comes from sloppy handling of citations.

---

14 **common knowledge:** information or ideas that anyone might be expected to know. *Christopher Columbus sailed to the New World in 1492* is common knowledge. *Columbus used knowledge of an upcoming lunar eclipse to terrify native Jamaicans into obedience* is not.

15 **plagiarism:** using someone else's words or ideas in writing without acknowledging the source. It's a form of stealing and can result in harsh consequences in both academic and professional writing. (For examples, see the reference section in the back of the book.)

8. Using a suitable reference style

    In citing sources, you can use parentheses, footnotes or endnotes, which are similar to footnotes but come at the end of the paper.[16] Often a list of all sources used in research is given at the end, whether cited in the paper or not. How you handle such referencing will depend on your purposes, what type of research you are doing, and what is expected by the person who will be reading the paper. If it's for school, your teacher will let you know what is expected. If it's performance data on the car you want to buy with a loan from your father, he'll simply want to know "according to whom?" If he's loaning you the money, he may well want to check your sources closely.

Two Things to Keep in Mind

Whether you are writing a persuasive essay, an expository piece, a narrative of some kind, or a research paper, it can be useful to keep the following in mind:

- Academic assignments are for learning. They are for *you*.
  Yes, you are writing for someone else to read it, but if it's an academic assignment, it should represent your learning. If you are writing for school but it doesn't represent any learning on your part, something is wrong.

- Writing is for communication. It is *your* communication.
  Don't get so caught up in the form of the piece or the expectations you think your teacher has that you forget to say what is important to you. Communicate what *you've* learned, what *you* see, what *you* know or believe.

> *Academic writing is only worthwhile when it represents your learning and your communication.*

---

16 Samples of different citation (documentation) styles are given in the reference section at the back of the book.

Part 4

TOOLS AND TIPS

This section covers tools and tips to
help make your writing stronger.

TONE

Tone is the attitude or feeling you adopt in your writing. For example, you could write in an aggressive tone or a friendly tone, an impartial tone or an interested tone, a scientific tone or a poetic tone.

One should consider the purpose and audience for the piece when deciding what tone to use. For example, an email to a friend will most likely be written in an informal, friendly tone. It can have shorter sentences, simpler vocabulary, and the personal pronoun, *you*.

Informal, friendly tone:

> *Hey Sophie, I'm having a party next weekend. Would you like to come?*
>
> *It's going to be really casual. Just come as you are and bring your favorite snack to share. Come to my place any time around 8 next Saturday night.*
>
> *Hope to see you then,*
>
> *Jennifer*

For comparison, a formal business document will have a distinctly different tone with more sophisticated words and sentences, and impersonal pronouns, such as *it* and *they*.

Formal, impartial, legal tone:

> *The Company shall reimburse Consultant for any reasonable costs and expenses incurred by Consultant in connection with the services performed by Consultant pursuant to the terms of this Agreement. Each such expenditure or cost shall be reimbursed.*

PART 4 TOOLS AND TIPS

Here's an excerpt from a modern nonfiction book. It adopts a professional, highly literate, but direct and interested tone:

> *The final and most important sign that we are succeeding will be that the term 'green' blessedly disappears. There will be no such thing as a green building, a green car, a green home, a green appliance, a green window, or even green energy. All those things will simply be the norm, because the ecosystem of prices, regulations, and performance standards will demand it.*
>
> Thomas L. Friedman

You can exercise your ability to assume different tones for nonfiction writing by creating several versions of a single piece, each in a different tone.

Your writing will communicate best when you use a tone that best suits your purpose and audience.

CONSISTENCY

Consistency in writing means having all elements work together harmoniously.

Here's an example showing lack of consistency:

> *I* woke up that morning and *we* knew it was going to be a great day. *I* grabbed *my* volleyball gear, headed to the gym and started *their* warm-up routine. *Our* teammates arrived in twos and threes.

This paragraph is confusing because it starts with *I*, *we* then back to *I* and *my*, then *their*, then switches to *our*. Who is being talked about?

Here's the same paragraph written with consistency:

> *I* woke up that morning and knew it was going to be a great day. *I* grabbed *my* volleyball gear, headed to the gym and started *my* warm-up routine. *My* teammates arrived in twos and threes.

Pronoun Consistency

As with the above example, consistency of pronouns means establishing the person (first, second or third) and number (singular or plural) and sticking with it throughout a piece or section.

Lack of pronoun consistency:

> When *they* heard about the opportunity to enter the writing contest and win a scholarship, *I* jumped at the chance. *You* know how hard it is to pay full college tuition. Their advisor had convinced *us* of that fact.

PART 4 TOOLS AND TIPS

Consistency of pronoun:

> When *I* heard about the opportunity to enter the writing contest and win a scholarship, *I* jumped at the chance. *I* knew how hard it would be to pay full college tuition. My advisor had convinced *me* of that fact.

You may need to use different pronouns throughout a piece of writing in some situations. This is expected and necessary. Nevertheless, within sections or paragraphs, inconsistency of pronouns can distract and confuse the reader, interrupting the smooth flow of ideas. It's something to watch for.

Tense Consistency

Consistency of tense (past, present, future) means establishing the main tense of a piece of writing and consistently using that throughout. Other tenses may be needed when switching the time frame for a specific reason, but to keep the tense consistent, return to the main tense as soon as possible.

Lack of tense consistency:

> As I *am sitting* on the patio sipping iced tea, there *was* a loud boom. I *realize* that I *will be running* toward the sound to see what *is causing* it, but I *have to put* on my shoes first. If anyone *is injured*, I *need* to call for help so I *grab* my cell phone and *ran* out the front door.

The italicized verbs show that this paragraph unnecessarily switches from present to past tense and even goes to future tense without any logical reason.

Consistency of tense:

> As I *was sitting* on the patio sipping iced tea, there *was* a loud boom. I *realized* that I should run toward the sound to see what *caused* it, but I *had to put* on my shoes first. I thought that if anyone *was injured*, I *would need* to call for help so I *grabbed* my cell phone and *ran* out the front door.

By sticking with the past tense, this paragraph is now easy to follow.

Tone Consistency

Consistency of tone means establishing the appropriate tone, manner and sophistication to suit the intended audience and sticking with it. For example, a student writing to other students may communicate best with a casual tone and language. A medical doctor writing a professional letter to other doctors would use a more formal tone. A magazine article or blog will use a tone consistent with that particular magazine or blog, and these can vary widely.

Lack of tone consistency:

> (For a school monthly magazine) As student council president, I would like to formally commend all participants in this year's telethon. Through the dedicated efforts of the project leaders and the thirty-two other people who participated, student government was able to raise over thirty thousand dollars toward upgrades of our art studio. It was really awesome! You guys rocked it!

This not only switches suddenly from a formal to an informal tone, it also switches from third person to second person in the last sentence, violating pronoun consistency.

Consistency of tone:

> (In an email to participants) The telethon was a fantastic success! I know a lot of you worked especially hard to bring it all together. Well, you really pulled it off. You raised $10,000 more than your target. Here's to your great new art studio. And thank you all!

Once you've decided on a tone to adopt for a piece of nonfiction writing, work to maintain consistency. Your readers will appreciate it and your communication will flow smoothly across.

Like good manners in verbal interaction,
consistency in writing assists the smooth transmission of ideas.

ACTIVE VS. PASSIVE

Verbs can be in various tenses. Here are the simplest examples.

    Present tense: Mimi *eats* apples.

    Past tense: Mimi *ate* apples yesterday.

    Future tense: Mimi *will eat* apples tomorrow.

Verbs change with singular and plural subjects.

    Singular: Mimi *eats* apples every day.

    Plural: Mimi and Carol *eat* apples every day.

Verbs can be transitive or intransitive.

    Transitive: Mimi *eats* apples every day.

    Intransitive: Mimi *eats* every day.

This chapter introduces what may be, to you, a new aspect of verbs. It is called **voice**. There are two types:

    Active voice: Mimi *eats* apples.

    Passive voice: Apples *are eaten* by Mimi.

A verb in **active voice** shows an action *caused by the subject*. A verb in **passive voice** shows an action *received by the subject*.

You may not have noticed or thought about these two different voices of verbs before. You may not have realized that you are often choosing between them when writing, but you are; and which voice you choose can make a difference in your writing.

PART 4 TOOLS AND TIPS

ACTIVE VOICE	PASSIVE VOICE
That lizard bit Joe!	*Joe was bitten by that lizard!*
The girl kicked the ball.	*The ball was kicked by the girl.*
She made a mistake.	*A mistake was made by her.*

The active versions and passive versions basically say the same thing, but they *feel* and *sound* different.

The difference is that in the active voice, the subject is *acting, causing* the action. (Lizard biting.) In the passive voice, the subject is being *affected by, allowing* or *receiving* the action. (Joe being bitten.)

As a general rule, you can write stronger, livelier sentences with the active voice. It's more direct and dynamic. In fact, strong writing prefers the active voice.

Why? The passive voice feels and sounds less committed, less certain, less direct.

This doesn't mean the passive voice doesn't have its uses, particularly when you want to avoid assigning responsibility for an action or want to emphasize something being acted upon or receiving an action, for example:

A mistake was made. (avoids assigning responsibility)

Seven ducklings were swept away in the flood. (emphasizes receipt of an action as opposed to the causing of an action)

As you begin to notice the use of active and passive voice in your writing or the writing of others, you may recognize that the passive voice often sounds more formal, more "educated," or more like news reporting.

Wheat has been grown for centuries by many cultures. (more "educated")

Today a free performance of James and the Giant Peach was given by the Children's Theater in Seattle. (like news reporting)

PART 4 TOOLS AND TIPS

One can be confused by the different names for clouds.
(more formal)

In active voice, these sentences would look like this:

For centuries, many cultures have grown wheat.

Today the Children's Theater gave a free performance of <u>James and the Giant Peach</u> in Seattle.

The different names for clouds can be confusing.

There's a reason passive voice sounds like reporting, or more "educated" or formal. It's because these types of writing are often done by someone trying to be objective and trying to avoid showing any bias or opinion.

That's why it feels less certain, less committed and less direct. And that's why it can be a problem if overdone or overused.

Passive: <u>Joe was told</u> he shouldn't go to the movies last night.

Active: <u>I told Joe</u> he shouldn't go to the movies last night.

Passive: <u>Our country was invaded</u> by the dictator on the first of May.

Active: <u>The dictator invaded our country</u> on the first of May.

Passive: <u>It was observed</u> by several scientists that <u>an unusual event was experienced</u> at the black hole last month.

Active: <u>Several scientists observed</u> an unusual event at the black hole last month. (rewording eliminated two uses of passive voice in the sentence)

In summary,

though it has its uses,
the passive voice is generally best avoided.[1]

---

[1] This sentence is in the passive voice! It's not illegal, just generally best avoided.

CONCRETE LANGUAGE

A sure way to have more impact in your writing is to use concrete language.

Concrete in writing means referring to physical objects, to things you can see, smell, hear, touch, taste or feel.

The opposite of concrete is abstract.

Abstract in writing means existing as an idea but not in a specific physical form.

Abstract language uses concepts you cannot perceive directly with your senses. Concrete language names real things you can see, smell, hear, touch, taste or feel. It gives your readers something they can "put their hands on." Here are some examples:

Abstract: *Happiness is <u>delightful</u>.*

Concrete: *Happiness is eating cold ice cream on a hot summer day.*

Abstract: *Colonizing Mars will be <u>problematic</u>.*

Concrete: *Mars has no air to breathe, water to drink, or plants to eat.*

Abstract: *We <u>love</u> the big tree in our yard.*

Concrete: *The majestic 80-foot oak in our front yard provides a shaded place for friends and neighbors to sit and talk on warm summer afternoons.*

There will always be abstract words and ideas in your writing, but they will carry more weight and meaning when assisted by concrete language that gives your reader distinct images.

PART 4 TOOLS AND TIPS

Here are further examples of abstract vs. concrete language:

ABSTRACT	CONCRETE
peace	soldiers putting down their arms
scared	visibly shaking from head to foot
friendliness	a hearty embrace
upset	shedding tears for fifteen minutes
lovely	sparkling eyes, welcoming smile
humorous	laughter bounced off the walls
fast	cheetah-like
courteous	spoke my name and shook my hand

Note that there can be different levels or degrees of concrete language. Some words or phrases are more concrete when compared to other words or phrases. The following can help illustrate this.

ABSTRACT   life

plant life

vegetable

green pepper

fried green chili pepper

CONCRETE   scorching mouthful of fried green chili pepper

The word *life* is abstract. It's an idea, not a physical thing. All the rest of the words or phrases, from *plant life* on down, are concrete. But as you move down the list, each one is more concrete than the one before.

PART 4 TOOLS AND TIPS

Grab a classic literature book like *The Wind in the Willows*, *The Hobbit*, or *Johnny Tremain* and read the first page or two. One reason why they have become classics is the use of concrete language.

*Using concrete language
will help you create vivid and lasting images.*

USAGE TIPS

Language is an ever-changing tool for the communication of ideas.

Many years ago, someone might have said "I happy-like accepted the present." Over time, the *like* got shortened to *ly*. Today we say, "I happily accepted the present."

Not very many years ago, this sentence would not have made sense: "She got so angry, she was like, 'Why would you ever say that!'" The word *like* went away from the end of words a long time ago, but recently it came back with a whole new meaning: it introduces a quotation.

Most new words or usages begin as informal. Some fade away after a while. Some gradually become accepted in more formal speech and writing. Some come into informal use and remain informal for a hundred years or more—they survive, but they never become accepted in formal speech and writing.

This new meaning of "like" may become accepted in formal speech and writing in another ten or twenty or thirty years. It may fade away. Or it may remain informal for a long time. Right now, it's used by many people, but it is still informal.

Much conversational English is informal. This can make it difficult to know when a term or phrase is informal because it seems to "sound right." Though the points that follow cover a range of usage tips, the majority address common informal usages that are best avoided in most business, professional or academic nonfiction writing.

accident/by accident

Another way to say that something happens *accidentally* is to say that it happens *by accident*. To say or write that something happens *on accident* is usually considered informal.

Avoid: *She called him "Bob" on accident.*

Instead: *She accidentally called him "Bob." Or, She called him "Bob" by accident.*

amount/number

In informal English, these two words are commonly used interchangeably, but they shouldn't be.

Amount refers to the quantity of something that cannot be counted or divided up into individual units:

A vast amount of water came ashore during the hurricane.

Number refers to a quantity of separate, individual units:

There were a number of baked potatoes on the platter.

Avoid: *I found a small amount of errors in his essay.*

Instead: *I found a small number of errors in his essay.*

and/or

And/or is rarely found in formal or professional writing. You can often just use *or*. If you want to be more exact, you can find a way to rewrite or add to the sentence.

Avoid: *Everyone attended and/or sent flowers.*

Instead: *Everyone either attended or sent flowers.*

or

Instead: *Everyone either attended or sent flowers; some did both.*

PART 4 TOOLS AND TIPS

cliché

A cliché is an expression that has been used so much that it no longer has the effectiveness it once had. They are best avoided in formal writing.

> EXAMPLES:
> That's cool.   raining cats and dogs
> fish out of water   fresh as a daisy
> I'm just saying.   sadder but wiser
> light as a feather   at the crack of dawn

Avoid: In *no way, shape or form* do I want him to take the car tonight.

Instead: I definitely do not want him to take the car tonight.

Your writing will have more impact if you explain or describe things your own way rather than depending on clichés.

et cetera (etc.)

Et cetera (from Latin) means *and other things* or *and the rest*. It is used at the end of a list of things to show that other things of the same type could be included. It is normally written in its abbreviated form, *etc.*

It is unnecessary to write *and etc.* because *and* is already in the meaning of *etc.*

In formal or professional writing, it is often avoided. It is easily replaced with *and so forth, and so on, and the like* or a simple phrase like the example below.

Avoid: You'll need paints, brushes, a canvas, rags, etc.

Instead: You'll need paints, brushes, a canvas, rags and similar supplies.

Note: The correct pronunciation is et SET uh ruh, not the common but incorrect ek SET uh ruh.

PART 4 TOOLS AND TIPS

fun as an adjective

In informal language, *fun* can be used to describe a person or thing:

> It was a *fun* day.
>
> Suki is a *fun* person.

This usage, however, is informal and best avoided.

In formal speech or writing, *fun* should only be used as a noun:

> I had *fun* today.
>
> Sierra is full of *fun*.
>
> It was *fun* learning how to prepare fancy desserts.

lay/lie

The verbs, *lay* and *lie*, are sometimes confused.

Lay means *to place (something)*.

> Please *lay* those logs by the fire.

Lie means *to recline*.

> She liked to *lie* and watch the reflections in the water.

With *lay*, there is always something receiving the action.

> I'll *lay* those bundles down for you.
>
> She *lays* her keys on the hall table.
>
> Ivana *laid* her bicycle under the porch.

With *lie*, there is nothing receiving the action. The subject reclines, rests, lounges or doesn't move.

> I told her to *lie* down and rest.
>
> She will *lie* on the couch until she feels better.
>
> I expect that book to *lie* there for at least another day before Sue remembers she left it.

PART 4 TOOLS AND TIPS

These words can become confused because the past of *lie* is *lay*.

> I *lie* on the floor today. I *lay* on the floor yesterday.

The past of *lay* is *laid*.

> Ivana *lays* her bicycle under the porch today. Ivana *laid* her bicycle under the porch yesterday.

These are all correct:

> She will lie down on the floor. (future)
>
> She lies down on the floor. (present)
>
> She lay down on the floor. (past)
>
> Tom will lay the book down. (future)
>
> Tom lays the book down. (present)
>
> Tom laid the book down. (past)

like/as

In informal English, *like* is often used when it would be correct to use *as*. *Like* means *similar to*. *As* means *in the same manner as*.

Avoid: I did it *like* my grandfather did.

Instead: I did it *as* my grandfather did.

These are all correct:

> It is a vehicle *like* a car. (similar to)
>
> She has a dress *like* mine. (similar to)
>
> He gave me several examples *like* the first one. (similar to)
>
> Jordan and Alex visited London, which was not *like* Paris or Rome. (similar to)
>
> Lily learned to cook *as* her grandmother did. (in the same manner as)

PART 4 TOOLS AND TIPS

> Cam did it *as* she had seen her mom do it. (in the same manner as)
>
> Do *as* I do, not *as* I say. (in the same manner as)

numbers spelled out

When you are writing, you often need to use numbers. The question becomes, "Do I write it as a numeral or do I spell it out?"

Different professional groups or publications use different rules, but the following are commonly agreed upon times you should spell out numbers in formal writing:

- numbers *one* through *ten*
- if it's only one or two words, such as a *million* or *two hundred* or *eighty-five*
- simple fractions, such as *three fourths* or *one half*
- starting a sentence, such as *Ninety-five* people attended the ceremony.
- first, second, third, and so on, such as The *first* thing I thought of, or the *thirty-seventh* time I asked, or the *fifth* chapter in the book.

On the other hand, there are times you should use numerals, not words:

- in scientific or technical reports (*12°C.*; *11.3* lbs.)
- dates (January *22, 1949*)
- time of day (*7:30* A.M.; *6:45* exactly)—except when using the term *o'clock*. We awoke at *eight* o'clock in the morning.
- common usage (World War *II*; Chapter *6*; Grade *5*; Verse *29*; Act *III*; pp. *29–31*; *54th* Street)

Above all, be consistent in your handling of numbers within a single piece of writing.

off of

The *of* in the phrase *off of* is unnecessary and not used in formal writing.

Avoid: He got *off of* the horse.

Instead: He got *off* the horse.

plus

The use of *plus* in place of *and* is informal.

Avoid: They went to town, ate a nice dinner, plus saw the new *Star Wars* movie.

Instead: They went to town, ate a nice dinner, and saw the new *Star Wars* movie.

pretty (as an adverb)

The use of *pretty* as an adverb is informal. It can often be omitted. It can also be replaced with *fairly, somewhat, quite* or *very,* depending on the intended meaning.

Avoid: The sisters are *pretty* close in age.

Instead: The sisters are close in age.

or

The sisters are *fairly* close in age.

Avoid: The knife wound was *pretty* deep.

Instead: The knife wound was deep.

or

The knife wound was *quite* deep.

PART 4 TOOLS AND TIPS

spelling, common confusions

- *accept/except*

  To *accept* something is to take it willingly.

  > I will happily *accept* gifts for my birthday.

  Except means *not including*.

  > Everyone is going *except* John.

- *affect/effect*

  To *affect* something is to change or influence it. It's a verb.

  > Lack of sleep *affected* his judgment.

  An *effect* is a result, something brought about. It's a noun.

  > Lack of sleep had an *effect* on his judgment.

  Less common, but correct English, *effect* can also be a verb, meaning *to make something happen, to bring about a result*.

  > The candidate promised to *effect* positive changes to the economy.

- *all right*

  The spelling *alright* is informal, except in written dialogue.

  > Avoid: It is *alright* if you go.
  >
  > Instead: It is *all right* if you go.

- *could of*

  The use of the word *of* after *could*, *should* or *might* is incorrect. It comes about because the "have" in the contractions *could've*, *should've* and *might've* sounds like "of." This is not an example of an informal use. It is simply incorrect.

  > Incorrect: I *could of* danced all night.
  >
  > Correct: I *could have* danced all night.

- *everyday/every day*

    Everyday is an adjective. It is used to say that something is common, ordinary or used in common, normal circumstances. When used this way, it comes before the noun.

    > It was just an *everyday* lunch—nothing special.

    > She wore her *everyday* coat, not her dressy one.

    When you want to describe an action that happens every day, the words are separate.

    > I have a protein drink *every day*.

    > Jan has a French class *every day* during the week.

- *supposed to*

    Supposed to is an idiom meaning *something is required or expected*. It is commonly misspelled *suppose to*.

    > Drivers are *supposed to* renew their licenses regularly.

    > Everyone is *supposed to* wash their dishes after dinner.

    > You are *supposed to* be my best friend and give me good advice.

spelling, compound words

A compound word is a word made up of two or more smaller words.

> *blackberry, cartwheel, everyday, setup, drop-kick, self-esteem, trigger-happy, father-in-law, seat belt, fine art, tongue twister*

Often compound words start off as two separate words, then over time become hyphenated. Some, in time, become combined into a single word. In the 1980s a person using the internet, which was new, would "go on-line." Today, people "go online."

Sometimes, two different spellings are accepted. Check a dictionary to be sure of the accepted spelling, or spellings, of a compound word.

PART 4 TOOLS AND TIPS

Compound adjectives used before a noun are hyphenated. The same words coming after a noun are normally written separately.

> The students took an off-campus trip on Wednesday.
>
> The students took a trip off campus on Wednesday.

than

The word *than* is used to compare things. "I'm taller *than* you. Sometimes, however, what is being compared can be unclear. To avoid this, supply the missing words that will make it clear.

Avoid: We like the cats more *than* the dogs. (Does this mean that we like the cats more than we like the dogs, or that we like the cats more than the dogs like the cats?)

Instead: We like the cats more *than* we like the dogs.

or

We like the cats more *than* the dogs do.

Avoid: My boyfriend cares more about social media *than* me.

Instead: My boyfriend cares more about social media *than* I do.

or

Instead: My boyfriend cares more about social media *than* he cares about me.

that

When *that* is used to connect groups of words, it can often be eliminated without changing the meaning of the sentence. For example, "I think (that) it will rain today." The sentence is correct with or without the *that*, but it is simpler without it.

On the other hand, you should be alert for the times when *that* is needed to make your meaning clear.

Avoid: When she first saw him, she felt his hair was his best feature. (The reader first sees "she felt his hair" and can get the wrong idea before continuing the sentence.)

Instead: When she first saw him, she felt *that* his hair was his best feature.

very

The use of *very* is often best avoided in formal writing. It's not incorrect or informal, just overused and usually unnecessary.

Avoid: I was very happy to hear the news.

Instead: I was happy to hear the news.

or

Instead: I was overjoyed to hear the news.

-wise

The use of the suffix *-wise* to turn nouns into modifiers came from military slang. It has never gained acceptance in formal writing so is best avoided.

Avoid: Size-*wise*, that door doesn't match specifications.

Instead: That door is the wrong size.

Avoid: That girl has what it takes to be a good player, skills-*wise*.

Standard: That girl has the skills needed to be a good player.

Part 5

CLARITY AND STYLE

This final section gives some guidance on improving clarity and developing your writing style.

FOUR ENEMIES OF CLARITY

This chapter takes up four major enemies to achieving clarity in writing.

Generalization

Generalization is making a statement about a group of people or things. The opposite of generalization is the use of specifics.

Though sometimes useful, generalizations often create problems by leaving the reader with an unclear picture or message. They can also leave the reader with doubt about the statement's truth.

Here's a generalization:

> Teenagers are unpredictable and unsafe drivers.

Here's a more specific statement:

> Nearly eighty percent of teenage drivers have a minor car accident in their first year of driving, but after that they have a better driving record than some other age groups, especially drivers seventy-five and older.

If you need to make a generalization, be sure to back it up with specific information. This will give readers a clear understanding of what you are trying to say and help you keep their trust in your message and conclusions.

Avoid generalizations. Be specific.

PART 5 CLARITY AND STYLE

Intensifiers

An **intensifier** is a modifier that intensifies the meaning of the word it modifies, making it stronger. Words like *so, very, such, quite, extremely* and *absolutely* are intensifiers.

For example:

> I *so* want you to meet him because he's *such* a nice man.

At first glance, these words would seem to be close friends of clarity, not enemies. After all, they help make the communication clearer, right?

Well, yes and no.

When intensifiers are overused, they can create the opposite effect to the one intended. A simple example will illustrate this. Compare the following sentences and decide for yourself which one is clearer and more believable:

> He is *really* a *very* honest man.
>
> He is an honest man.

Most would agree that the second is clearer and more believable.

You can learn a lot by taking a piece of your writing and eliminating all the intensifiers. Alternatively, you can take some writing and add many intensifiers to see what effect it has on clarity.

> *Improve clarity by using intensifiers sparingly.*

Overstatement

Overstatement is exaggeration. It's a description or statement that is too strong, too emotional or too serious to be easily accepted.

Overstatement is when a whole sentence, paragraph, section or piece of writing acts like an intensifier. In attempting to make a message stronger, the writer has gone too far:

> *The democrats will do anything to hold their Congressional seats.*
>
> *My sister has never said a kind word to me her entire life.*
>
> *Everyone in attendance burst into tears at the end of the talk.*

Overstatements often begin with objective facts or truth, but then wander off in the direction of fiction. They can instantly destroy any trust in the writer.

Many examples of overstatement can be found, unfortunately, in political discourse. If you've ever found yourself reacting badly to a political argument, debate or speech, it may have been due to the repeated use of overstatement, as in the "democrats will do anything" example above.

You may have noticed that this "democrats" example is also a generalization: "The democrats" means "all democrats." Intensifiers, generalizations and overstatement often team up to defeat your attempts at clarity. Compare the following:

> *My dad is absolutely the world's very best agriculturalist. He grows extremely large apples that weigh as much as watermelons.*
>
> *My dad has been experimenting with agricultural techniques for years. Last year, he grew several apples that weighed over three pounds each.*

> *To maintain trust, avoid overstatement.*

PART 5 CLARITY AND STYLE

Weak Statements

The last of our four enemies to clarity is the weak statement. This is when, for whatever reason, you avoid stating something definitely and positively. It can be that you aren't sure of your opinion or your information, or simply that you aren't willing to commit to your message.

Whatever the reason for using weak statements, your writing will only suffer.

> *I guess you could say that Dorn Hall was not as nice as some places. You would almost have thought that the cleaning personnel didn't care all that much about what they were supposed to be doing. It's not that they weren't nice people, although that point might have been somewhat open to question, but just that they were less than thorough about their jobs. In my opinion, it would have been a bit better to hire people who wanted to put a little more time and effort into the cleaning.*

There is nothing technically wrong with this paragraph. It even has a certain style that is casual and forgiving. But let's compare it with this:

> *Dorn Hall was filthy, and the cleaning personnel were rude and incompetent. If I'd been the landlord, I would have fired the lot of them within a week.*

One sign of noncommittal writing is too many words. Strong, definite statements are usually short and to the point.

There will be times when you want to acknowledge uncertainty or lack of agreement. And being overly definite can come across as overstatement. The trick is to get good at spotting weak statements and uncovering the reason for them. If you need to do more research to be sure of what you are saying, do so. If you need to find more courage to be definite in your views, find it. If you simply need to take out all the qualifying phrases, take them out.

Avoid weak statements by being sure and definite.
The result will be improved clarity.

DEVELOPING A STYLE

Style, in the most general sense, is the way something is done or expressed. For example, there are different styles of teaching, different styles of painting, different styles of singing.

A more specific meaning of **style** is this: the characteristic way that a writer uses language.

Every writer chooses words and composes sentences and paragraphs in their own way, and that is their style.

For example, here are excerpts from two renowned American authors:

> "I like to listen. I have learned a great deal from listening carefully. Most people never listen."
>
> Ernest Hemingway

> "On the day before Thanksgiving, toward the end of the afternoon, having motored all day, I arrived home and lit a fire in the living room. The birch logs took hold briskly. About three minutes later, not to be outdone, the chimney itself caught fire...."
>
> E.B. White

Each of these successful writers knew the same basic rules and guidelines of sentences, paragraphs, grammar and punctuation in English. They had access to the same English vocabulary. But the things they had to say, and the way they chose to say them, were widely different.

They each surely read millions of words of others' writing. And they each wrote millions of words of their own. Along the way, each developed a style unique to himself. Just as you may be able to easily

PART 5 CLARITY AND STYLE

recognize a particular singer after hearing just a few notes, some can recognize a writer after just a few sentences or paragraphs.

That's *style*.

Most people can sing. Most people can run. Everyone can laugh. Yet no two people sing, run or laugh exactly the same way.

You can try singing, running or laughing different ways, but eventually you will settle into a way that is clearly *you*. So it is with writing. You develop a writing style by doing a lot of writing—and a lot of reading.

Early on, focus on knowing what you want to say and saying it in the way you think is most effective. Use what you've learned, experiment and try new things. Notice what other writers do and how they do it.

Over time, your own "voice" or style will emerge. You may even find confidence in two, three or more different styles, all of which feel true to you.

> *When your writing becomes a natural and effortless expression of you, you will have acquired a writing style.*

Good luck, and happy adventures with nonfiction writing!

REFERENCE SECTION

COMMON STANDARDS & USAGE SAMPLES

COMMON STANDARDS & USAGE SAMPLES

Academic Writing Format

Standards for formatting academic assignments can vary according to the type of assignment, the school and the teacher. Here are common expectations.

1. Heading including name, date, and name of the course for which the paper is being written. Certain teachers may request these in a particular order or presentation. The title should be centered just above the body of the paper.

2. Assignment name. Sometimes, the full wording of the assignment is expected, often with the course and step number or class. Make it easy for anyone reading it to know what they are reading.

3. Margins and format. Generally, leave one inch on all sides of the paper. Left align the text. Double space or 2.0 spacing throughout the paper. Do not add extra space above or below the title of the paper or between paragraphs. Indent the first line of each paragraph 1/2 inch from the left margin. If there's another specific format required by the teacher or school, follow that.

4. Paper size and quality. The normal expectation is 8½ x 11 white paper. If handwritten on lined paper, be sure to avoid ragged edges, such as those torn out of a spiral notebook.

5. Writing and font. If handwritten, clearly legible writing in blue or black ink is the normal expectation. If typed (word processed and printed), it's best to use a single, common 12-point font, unless the instructor specifies a different font size.

COMMON STANDARDS & USAGE SAMPLES

Jay Jones

Oceanography 201

Professor Marks

20 March 2023

Research step 12: Do a research project on a topic of interest and document your findings in a paper of at least 1500 words.

Tackling the Ocean

    It had always been a mystery to me why certain locations on the nearby California coast were better for surfing than others. I knew the underwater slope was a factor and obviously one needs safe access to the waves and can't be worried about crashing into rocky outcroppings on the shore. But why were some spots so consistently good for beginning and intermediate surfers, while others were not? ... (and so on)

COMMON STANDARDS & USAGE SAMPLES

Outlines

Though your teacher, school or class may have specific expectations, there are usual, accepted ways to write outlines. One type is called a *sentence outline*, as it uses full sentences. Another is called a *topic outline*, as it just states topics. It is best to choose one or the other and be consistent throughout the outline. Following are samples of each.

Sentence Outline

I. Introduction: The country of Nepal is making progress in protecting tigers.

II. Tigers are the largest cats, valued for their strength.
    a. They are up to 6 feet long and can run 50 km/hour.
    b. They hunt other large animals, alone, after dark.
        i. They can kill and drag prey five times their size.
        ii. After killing a large animal, they may hunt only once that week.

III. Tigers are endangered.
    a. Their bones, whiskers, teeth and eyes are used in Chinese medicine.
    b. Criminals make lots of money illegally killing tigers.
    c. As human civilization spreads, tigers have less wild country to live in.
    d. There are only about 4,000 tigers in the wild.

IV. Several countries have rescue programs.
    a. There are fines for illegally killing tigers.
    b. Countries with tigers have park rangers patrolling.
    c. Rangers remove traps and try to catch illegal tiger hunters.

V. Conclusion: In Nepal they have been successful.
    a. They have created paths between parks so tigers can move around safely.

COMMON STANDARDS & USAGE SAMPLES

    b. Private groups help the government study and protect tigers.

    c. There has been a tiger population increase over the past few years.

Topic Outline

I. **Introduction: Dogs are better pets than cats.**

II. **Cats are easy to care for**
    A. Cats are independent
        1. Eating habits
        2. Need for companionship
        3. Bathroom habits
    B. Cats are clean

III. **Dogs are companions**
    A. Communicate with owners
        1. Always affectionate
        2. Attuned to owner's emotions
    B. Protect owners

IV. **Comparison of cats versus dogs**
    A. Cats need less but give less
    B. Dogs need more care but provide more
        1. Companionship
        2. Opportunity to exercise
        3. Protection

V. **Conclusion: Dogs make better pets for those who want productive companions.**

Word processors offer different outline formats. The ones used in these examples are commonly used.

Note that any part of the outline will logically have more than one entry. Using the above, there is no A without a B or 1 without a 2.

COMMON STANDARDS & USAGE SAMPLES

Research Documentation

Documentation can be done with footnotes; however, it is more commonly done today with parenthetical information, which is easier and less cumbersome.

Depending on the school, teacher or assignment, you may need to be exact in your format with either method. Regardless, be sure to give the reader all the information necessary to find the exact source.

The Modern Language Association (MLA) provides agreed-upon standards for the use of parenthetical documentation, footnotes and works cited lists. If these standards are expected, refer to a text or site that covers the details of how it is currently done, as they are evolving.

Here are three examples showing different ways to document sources of information.

1. The following is from a research paper discussing the pros and cons of artificial intelligence in homes, quoting information from an article in *The Atlantic* magazine. This is documented according to MLA standards, so the author and page number are noted. Then the full information on that source is provided in the "Works Cited" list at the end of the paper (listed in alphabetical order by author's last name). A quotation of more than four lines is usually shown as follows, indented and without quotation marks.

    Should we be concerned about privacy with artificial intelligence devices in our homes? Here's one view:

    > The speakers' manufacturers promise that only speech that follows the wake word is archived in the cloud, and Amazon and Google, at least, make deleting those exchanges easy enough. Nonetheless, every so often weird glitches occur, like the time Alexa recorded a family's private conversation without their having said the wake word and emailed the recording to an acquaintance on their contacts list. Amazon explained that Alexa must have been awakened by a word that sounded like Alexa (*Texas? A Lexus? Praxis?*), then misconstrued elements of the ensuing conversation as a

COMMON STANDARDS & USAGE SAMPLES

> series of commands. The explanation did not make me feel much better. (Shulevitz 4)

WORKS CITED

Shulevitz, Judith. "Alexa, Should We Trust You?" *The Atlantic*, The Atlantic Monthly Group, November 2018. Print.

Note: *Print* means you are quoting from a paper copy of the book or magazine. If the book or magazine article is found online, you would replace *Print* with *Web* and the date found.

2. For a shorter quote in a less formal piece that does not include a "Works cited" page, the parenthetical information should be placed immediately after the quote and be able to stand alone. Quotation marks are used.

   > "Alexa's manufacturers promise that only speech that follows the wake word is archived in the cloud, and Amazon and Google, at least, make deleting those exchanges easy enough." (Judith Shulevitz, "Alexa, Should We Trust You?" *The Atlantic* magazine, November 2018. Web. 11 Feb 2020.)

3. The following excerpt from a research paper about Iceland's economic collapse in 2008 uses a phrase first to introduce the source of information and a footnote to cite the full data about that source.

   > In his book *Hot, Flat, and Crowded*, Thomas L. Friedman provides an example of a warped economy:
   >
   > > In 2003, Iceland…became one big, wild offshore bank…. The country's entire economy got warped. Students fled from traditional careers in fishing or engineering for the economics of making money from money. When the laws of gravity finally kicked in and Iceland's three new global-size banks collapsed in October 2008, Iceland's 300,000 citizens found that they were responsible for $100 billion of banking losses—which works out to roughly $330,000 for every Icelandic man, woman, and child.[1]

---

[1] Friedman, Thomas L. *Hot, Flat, and Crowded, Why We Need a Green Revolution and How It Can Renew America*. New York: Picador, December 2009.

COMMON STANDARDS & USAGE SAMPLES

Plagiarism

If not common knowledge, the source of information should be clearly cited. The following examples are provided for illustration.

Source:

> "Whether it is used for everyday talking or for singing an operatic aria, for shouting or for whispering, the human voice is an amazing sound producer. It involves the throat, mouth, nose, and chest to produce its remarkable range of sounds." —*The Science of Music* by Melvin Berger

Plagiarism by copying:

> When *it is used for everyday talking and for singing, for shouting and* for whispering, the voice is an amazing sound producer. *It* makes sounds using *the throat, mouth, nose, and chest.* With these, it can *produce its remarkable range of sounds.*

Not plagiarism:

> I believe the human voice is truly unique. Melvin Berger describes it this way: "[T]he human voice is an amazing sound producer. It involves the throat, mouth, nose, and chest to produce its remarkable range of sounds." (*The Science of Music* 10)

Plagiarism by paraphrasing:

> The human voice can be used to make many amazing sounds such as talking, singing, yelling or whispering. However it is used, it makes incredible sounds using the mouth, throat, nose and chest. I used to believe the mouth and throat were the only things needed to produce the remarkable range of sounds.

Not plagiarism:

> As Melvin Berger discusses in his book *The Science of Music*, the human voice produces its impressive variety of sounds by using not just the throat and mouth but also the nose and chest. I had always believed the mouth and throat were the only things involved in making vocal sounds, but I have come to learn the importance of the nose and chest as well.

COMMON STANDARDS & USAGE SAMPLES

The following give examples of information that would require documentation versus information that would not.

NOT COMMON KNOWLEDGE REQUIRES DOCUMENTATION	COMMON KNOWLEDGE DOES NOT REQUIRE DOCUMENTATION
a project undertaken in 2012 by the Homeland Security Department	when the US Homeland Security Department was established
a research breakthrough on treating cancer	the existence of cancer
a quote from a Dickens' novel, "A Merry Christmas, uncle." …. "Bah, humbug!" said Scrooge.	that Dickens wrote a novel entitled *A Christmas Carol*
a statement from a presidential candidate	the names of the candidates in a presidential election
An elephant researcher finds how babies are raised by their mothers.	Elephants travel in herds.
An economist studies cost of living statistics in Europe and draws a conclusion.	The cost of living is rising in Europe.
specific arguments in an impeachment trial	that the U.S. President is being impeached
The Roman emperors Augustus, Caligula, and Trajan all ordered aqueducts built.	The Romans built aqueducts in Europe.
70% of their writing grads have writing careers	U. Mass at Amherst is known for their excellent writing program.

COMMON STANDARDS & USAGE SAMPLES

Personal Letters

Here's a sample personal letter showing the format of the letter and the mailing envelope.

> 5401 Pine Street
> Manchester, MA 01944
>
> April 21, 2019
>
> Dear Aunt Claire,
>
> Thank you for the birthday present! A new tablet will be incredibly useful. I am already using it for reading my school literature assignments, sending and receiving emails, doing research and listening to my favorite music.
>
> At the coast over the weekend, I got an idea for an article for the school newspaper. I was able to start the research and writing right away because of my new tablet! I will email a copy to you when I'm done. I hope you like it.
>
> Thanks again. It was a thoughtful gift that I'll use for years.
>
> With love,
> Christine

Christine Boulet
5401 Pine Street
Manchester, MA. 01944

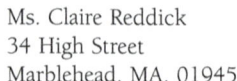

Ms. Claire Reddick
34 High Street
Marblehead, MA. 01945

COMMON STANDARDS & USAGE SAMPLES

Business Letters

Here's a sample business letter showing the format of the letter and the mailing envelope.

35 SW Moorland Hill Rd
Portland, Oregon 97204
(503) 123-4567

March 12, 2023

Daniel J. McCarthy
CEO Frontier Communications
401 Merritt St.
Norwalk, CT 06851

Re: Spoofers and Hackers

Dear Mr. McCarthy:

I am writing to Frontier because, as my service provider, you are the central player and my representative for the telecommunications system as it is administered in the United States. That system is failing me.

Today, I have received four calls from criminals seeking my credit card information. In all cases, the phone number that appeared on my caller ID was from my local exchange. I live in Portland, Oregon. Obviously, they are not operating locally... (and so on)

Sincerely,

Jill Smith
Jill Smith

Jill Smith
35 SW Moorland Hill Road
Portland, Oregon 97204

Daniel J. McCarthy
CEO Frontier Communications
401 Merritt St.
Norwalk, CT 06851

COMMON STANDARDS & USAGE SAMPLES

Transitions

Common transition words and phrases:

thus	though	finally	because of this
otherwise	again	therefore	for example
besides	as a result	for instance	similarly
so	specifically	in this way	even though
then	however	next	for this reason
in conclusion	in addition	above all	in other words

Sample of a transition phrase that helps connect two sentences:

> Teng learned to read music at a young age. As a result, in high school he could easily look over a piece of music and get an idea what it would sound like.

Sample of a transition that helps connect two paragraphs:

> The Nepalese government has tried but has found it difficult to control illegal tiger hunting.
>
> Even though the government of Nepal has not been able to stop the illegal hunting of tigers entirely, they have made great progress....

Sample sentences showing how different transition words change the meaning. (Each would fit a different context, of course.)

> Heather came to the end of the garden. As a result, she saw that the gate was locked.
>
> Heather came to the end of the garden. Again, she saw that the gate was locked.
>
> Heather came to the end of the garden. Specifically, she saw that the gate was locked.
>
> Heather came to the end of the garden. She saw, however, that the gate was locked.
>
> Heather came to the end of the garden. In other words, she saw that the gate was locked.

GLOSSARY

A

abstract language
Abstract means existing as an idea but not in a specified physical form. *Abstract language* uses concepts you cannot perceive directly with your senses, such as: *peace, scared, friendliness.*

argument
In persuasive writing, the set of reasons that support your opinion, point or proposal. The term *argument* can also be used to refer to one of the points supporting your thesis, instead of the whole set of points.

B

body
The series of paragraphs that comprise the majority of the piece. The body of a piece takes the reader through a sequence of ideas that make your overall point or deliver your overall message. Sometimes called the *story.*

brevity
The quality of being brief, short or concise. In speech or writing, it means using just the words needed, no more.

C

cite (a reference or person)
To quote or refer to information from someone else, particularly when it supports some point or argument you are making.

GLOSSARY

coach
   Anyone providing feedback that includes responsibility for helping the student improve his or her writing.

common knowledge
   Information or ideas that anyone might be expected to know. *Christopher Columbus sailed to the New World in 1492* is common knowledge. *Columbus used knowledge of an upcoming lunar eclipse to terrify native Jamaicans into obedience* is not common knowledge.

con
   Short for *contra* (which means "against"). A *con* is a point that disagrees with and refutes the thesis. It is used mainly in the phrase *pros and cons.* Also called *counterargument.*

conclusion
   The end of a piece where you bring your reader to the final destination, arrive to the overall message or point, and effectively close the piece of writing. Sometimes called the *close.*

concrete language
   Concrete in writing means referring to physical objects as opposed to abstract ideas. *Concrete language* names real things you can see, smell, hear, touch, taste, or feel, such as *a hearty embrace, shedding tears for fifteen minutes, sparkling eyes.*

consistency
   Consistency in writing means having all elements (such as pronouns, tense and tone) working together harmoniously.

consistency of pronouns
   Establishing the person (first, second or third) and number (singular or plural) and sticking with it throughout a piece or section.

consistency of tense
   Establishing the main tense of a piece of writing and consistently using that throughout. Other tenses may be needed when switching the time frame for a specific reason, but to keep the tense consistent, one returns to the main tense as soon as possible.

GLOSSARY

consistency of tone
Establishing the appropriate tone, manner, and sophistication to suit the intended audience and sticking with it.

counterargument
Any point opposing your thesis. See *con*.

CV or *Curriculum Vitae*
(Latin for "course of life") similar to a *résumé*, but with a longer summary of experience emphasizing academic achievements and degrees. It is commonly used when applying for higher academic or research opportunities or positions. Sometimes the terms *résumé* and *CV* are used interchangeably.

D

descriptive writing
Writing that describes something in detail, such as a person, place, thing, or event.

documentation
Citing of sources.

draft, first
The first version of a piece of writing before any revising is done.

E

essay
A short piece of writing on a subject, usually presenting the writer's personal views.

expository writing
Writing that "exposes," explains or brings something into open view.

GLOSSARY

F

feedback
Information on how well you are doing something given for the purpose of improving your performance. *Feedback* on a piece of writing is what someone has to say about how well your writing communicates, what was understandable, effective, confusing or unclear.

fiction
Writing that is a product of the imagination rather than being based on fact. Novels and some short stories, plays and poems are examples of fiction writing.

G

generalization
Making a statement about a group of people or things, such as "teenagers are unpredictable and unsafe drivers."

I

intensifier
A modifier that intensifies the meaning of the word it modifies, making it stronger. Words like *so, very, such, quite, extremely* and *absolutely* are intensifiers.

introduction
A beginning to a piece of writing that is a way to bring the reader smoothly into the topic and launch them on the path you intend to take them down. Sometimes called the *lead*.

N

narrative writing
Narrate means *tell a story*. Writing that recounts an event or sequence of events is narrative writing.

GLOSSARY

nonfiction writing
Writing about real people, real places, real events. It can come in many forms: books, essays, articles, blogs, reports, proposals, short stories, biographies, autobiographies, scientific or other technical papers, and more.

O

overstatement
An exaggeration; a description or statement that is too strong, too emotional or too serious to be easily accepted.

P

paragraph
A group of sentences that addresses one main idea. Occasionally, a paragraph is a single sentence. Regardless of length, paragraphs are the main building blocks of pieces of writing.

persuasive writing
To *persuade* is to say things that will get someone to agree with a certain view or take a certain action. Persuasive writing should start with a statement of the opinion being proposed or the problem being addressed and persuade the reader to agree with the writer's view.

piece
A single creation of art, music or writing. In writing, a *piece* can be an essay, an article or any other composition.

plagiarism
Using someone else's words or ideas in writing without acknowledging the source. It's a form of stealing and can result in harsh consequences in both academic and professional writing.

postulate:
Something put forth as a truth to act as a starting point for investigation or discussion.

GLOSSARY

pro
In a persuasive essay, *pros* are the points that agree with and support the thesis. It is used mainly in the phrase *pros and cons.*

proofreading
Reading something written to find and mark errors for correction.

R

refining
Making more detailed changes to sharpen the writing. Done after revising, refining is done to "purify" your writing of any illogical or inexact ideas, wordiness, and so on, making it clear and enjoyable to read.

report
A description or telling about something that happened or the results of an investigation. The goal is to inform, but the purpose of a report should be more specific, such as giving the reader a more accurate view into some subject or event, or presenting facts in a certain way that point to what's important about them or what conclusions you have drawn from them.

research
An investigation into some part of life in order to make new observations and conclusions, or to find solutions to problems. It usually includes study of the observations and conclusions made by others. Its purpose is new discoveries, insights or answers, even if only new to oneself.

research paper
An accurate written report of research done and the conclusions reached.

résumé
A summary of educational, professional and other work experience qualifications for a job. It is accompanied by a brief cover letter requesting an interview.

GLOSSARY

revising
Revising means examining and changing your writing to improve it.

run-on sentence
Two or more complete sentences put together without a conjunction or correct punctuation.

S

sentence
A group of words that has a subject and its verb, and that expresses a complete thought. It can be simple or complicated, short or long. It can have multiple subjects, verbs and descriptive phrases.

sentence fragment
A fragment is a small piece of something. A sentence fragment is a piece of a sentence written *as if it were* a sentence. It is *not* a complete sentence because it lacks a subject or its verb, or it does not express a complete thought.

style
Generally, the way something is done or expressed, such as different styles of teaching, different styles of painting, different styles of singing. In writing, style is the characteristic way that a writer uses language.

T

thesis
The main point or opinion in a written assignment, normally introduced at or near the beginning. It is assumed that a thesis is worth writing about, that it is a specific and independent idea requiring some persuasion.

tone
The attitude or feeling you adopt in your writing.

transition
A word or group of words that helps connect sentences or paragraphs together, such as *thus, however, for this reason,* or *because of this.*

GLOSSARY

V

Voice

Voice in grammar refers to the action being caused by the subject or received by the subject.

A verb in *active voice* shows an action *caused by the subject*.

> *That lizard bit Joe!*
>
> *The girl kicked the ball.*
>
> *She made a mistake.*

A verb in *passive voice* shows an action *received by the subject*.

> *Joe was bitten by that lizard!*
>
> *The ball was kicked by the girl.*
>
> *A mistake was made by her.*

INDEX

A

abstract language
  definition, 85
  examples, 85
argument
  definition in persuasive
      writing, 51
audience
  choice of words, examples, 7
  define, 7
  define before starting writing, 7

B

body (or story), 45
business letter
  explains a request or need, 59
  sample, Reference Section, 121
business writing
  make your point efficiently, 57

C

coaching
  definition, 18
  examples, 19
  tips, 18

common knowledge, 70
conclusion (or close), 45
concrete language
  definition, 85
  examples, 85
cons
  definition, 51
  foundation for supporting
      points, 52
  start with cons in argument, 51
consistency
  definition, 77
  of pronouns, 77
  of tense, 78
  of tone, 79
Curriculum Vitae
  definition, 58

D

deductive reasoning
  definition, 65
descriptive writing
  describes in detail, 62
  examples, 62
documentation
  definition, 70
  examples, Reference Section, 116

131

INDEX

draft
  definition of first draft, 11
  goal for first draft, 11
  tips to get started, 11
  ways to improve, 13

E

expository writing
  examples, 62
  provides information, not opinion, 61

F

feedback
  definition, 17
finishing
  proofreading, 22
  questions to ask, 22
  standard, 21

G

generalization, 103

I

inductive reasoning
  definition, 64
intensifiers
  overuse, 104
introduction (or lead), 43

L

language
  avoid using informal, 28

N

narrative writing
  can use elements of storytelling, 63
  definition, 63
  examples, 63
nonfiction writing
  definition, 1
  goal to inform the reader, 5
  purpose, 5

O

outline
  complex piece of writing, 9
  definition, 9
  organizing steps, 9
  organizing tips, 9
  professional, 10
  sample, Reference Section, 114
overstatement, 105

P

paragraphs
  continuity, 40
  definition, 39
  integrity, 40
  length, 39
personal writing
  focus on key points, 55
  sample, Reference Section, 120
  uses, 55
persuasive essays
  develop critical thinking, 61
  use thesis, pros and cons to conclusion, 61

INDEX

persuasive writing
  from thesis to argument to conclusion, 54
  uses, 49
plagiarism
  definition, 70
  what requires documentation, 119
pretty (as an adverb), 95
proofreading
  definition, 22
  tips, 23
proposal, professional
  key elements, 57
pros
  definition, 51
purpose
  before you start writing, 5
  clarify, 6
  document or recreate an event, 5
  introduce viewpoint, 5
  letter, email, or post, 6
  persuade, 5
  present series of facts, 6
  research report, 6

R

refining
  definition, 15
  how to, 15
report
  purpose, 6
research
  different approaches in reasoning, 64

research documentation
  examples, 116
  styles, 116
research paper
  documentation, 70
  key elements, 68
  purpose, 67
résumé
  definition, 58
  tips, 58
revising
  definition, 14
  how to, 14

S

sections
  body (or story), 45
  conclusion (or close), 45
  description, 43
  introduction (or lead), 43
sentences
  concise, 36
  definition, 31
  different importance, 36
  fragment, 32
  great ones, 37
  important sentences or words placed last, 36
  rhythm and variety, 34
  run-on, 33
style
  definition in writing, 107
  developing a writing style, 108

INDEX

T

thesis
 definition, 49
 idea requiring persuasion, 49
 tips for developing, 50
tone
 definition, 75
 formal characteristics, 75
 informal characteristics, 75
 suit purpose and audience, 76
transition words and phrases
 common, Reference Section, 122
 definition, 15

U

unnecessary words
 describing words, 28
 prepositions, 28
 that repeat something already stated, 29
 wordy phrases, 29

V

voice
 active, 81
 passive, 81
 use of active, 82
 use of passive, 82

W

weak statements, 106
words
 avoid informal language, 28
 avoid overusing a word, 28
 avoid unnecessary fancy words, 28
 don't over-explain, 27
 don't use you aren't certain of, 27
 eliminate unnecessary words, 28
 use words your reader will understand, 27
writing
 format, Reference Section, 113
 purpose for each piece, 5

www.ingramcontent.com/pod-product-compliance
Lightning Source LLC
Chambersburg PA
CBHW081200230426
43666CB00016B/2873